Make the Most of a Good Thing: YOU!

Make the Most of a Good Thing: YOU!

by Diana Shaw

Joy Street Books
Little, Brown and Company
Boston   Toronto

THIRD HARDCOVER PRINTING
PAPERBACK EDITION PUBLISHED 1987

Library of Congress Cataloging-in-Publication Data

Shaw, Diana.
  Make the most of a good thing, you!

  Bibliography: p.
  Summary: Offers the adolescent girl advice on sexual
changes in the body, diet and nourishment, exercise,
dealing with stress, and staying healthy.
  1. Adolescent girls—Health and hygiene—Juvenile
literature. 2. Health—Juvenile literature.
[1. Adolescent girls Health and hygiene. 2. Health]
I. Title.
RA778.S547 1985   613'.04243   85-71372
ISBN 0-316-78340-4(hc)
ISBN 0-316-78342-0 (pb)

Illustrations on pages 14 and 15 by Mark Lefkowitz

BP

Published simultaneously in Canada

PRINTED IN THE UNITED STATES OF AMERICA

For Missy

Contents

Acknowledgments

Many thanks to those authorities who lent their time and expertise to this book: Dr. Gloria Castle of Los Angeles Children's Hospital; William B. Hansen, C. Kevin Malotte, Shelley Mann, and Louise Hane of the Mark Taper Center for Health Enhancement at UCLA; Nancy Jane Benfield; and the girls in Judith Selsor's eighth-grade study hall at Walter Reed Junior High School.

Thanks to Kelly Goode, whose careful readings, tactful advice, and unfailing enthusiasm propelled me and the manuscript through this process. Thanks also to Melanie Kroupa, Amy Meeker, and Carolyn Perot, my Atlantic editors, whose scrupulous work and imaginative suggestions strengthened each draft; and to my agent, Janet Manus, who provided the coddling and encouragement most writers need but seldom get so regularly and abundantly.

Thanks to my cover girls: Jenny Hughes, Tanya

Gagliano, Lynn Hayakawa, Michele Wilson, Rebecca Bain, Vanessa DeCarvalho, Keishila Jones, and Jonetta Thomas, for giving me the look I wanted for this book.

Make the Most of a Good Thing:
YOU!

Introduction

What's New about You

"I hate my hair!"
"My skin is so gross!"
"I'm getting so fat!"
Sound familiar? Maybe you haven't had much
good to say about your body lately. Maybe your
face isn't as smooth as you would like it to be.
Maybe you're fat where you used to be thin.
Maybe you think your breasts look funny. And
maybe all of this makes you feel that you're help-
lessly hopeless.

You're not. Your body is changing, but there is
plenty you can do to help make it change for the
better.

It's not hard to find advice on how to lose
weight, clear up your skin, or get your body in
shape. It's everywhere you look. The trouble is
that most of it is meant for women whose bodies
have already gone through the changes that yours
is going through now. As you'll discover in this

book, your body, because it's developing, has special needs that older women no longer have.

This book will teach you how to take care of your body while it's changing and show you that you can control much about the way you look and feel. It will give you the information, advice, and guidance you'll need to make your body become the best it can be.

More Than Skin-Deep

At its best, your body will be energetic enough to do everything you have to do and everything you want to do. You'll recover easily when you get sick, and you'll be able to handle whatever problems may come up at home or at school.

It's important to keep in mind that when it's at its best, your body will be different — maybe *very* different — from your best friend's body or the body of your favorite model, actress, or athlete. To be good, a body doesn't have to look a particular way or perform any special feats. It *does* have to keep you going, and it should be able to give you pleasure and confidence.

Good Care, Lasting Care

The kind of care you give your body now, while it's developing, will be the key to lasting good health and good looks. Doctors have recently found that your health habits and attitudes during adolescence (the time between childhood and full-fledged womanhood) affect you for the rest of your life. Getting into good eating and exercise habits, and developing confidence in yourself right now, will make all the difference in the way you look and feel today *and* in all of the years to come.

Health First

You develop a good body by learning what it takes to keep *yourself* healthy, not by trying to look like someone else. If you worry just about your looks, you may actually ruin your chances to look good, and you definitely risk your chances of feeling good. Trying to starve yourself into shape, instead of controlling your weight by eating well and exercising often, may make you thinner, but you'll risk developing unattractive symptoms of malnourishment: limp hair, dry skin, dull eyes, and lousy moods. Trying to cover your zits with heavy makeup instead of treating them by eating wholesome foods and getting lots of fresh air may only make you end up with more of them.

Making It Work for You

As you read through this book you'll get to know what kinds of foods, exercises, and attitudes will help you look and feel your best. Just as important, you'll find out how to make them part of your life. (Everyone knows it's one thing to understand what you're supposed to do, and another thing to get yourself to do it.)

For example, you'll learn which foods are best for you, *and* how to deal with family and friends who make it tough to eat the way you should. Besides learning how cigarettes and alcohol can hurt you, you'll learn how to get out of situations where you're expected to smoke or drink.

In addition to learning why exercise keeps you in good shape and high spirits, you'll find out how to choose the kind of exercise you'll want to do every day.

You Are in Charge

The most important piece of information in this book doesn't appear in any single chapter or section. It's a message that runs through the entire book: *you* are in charge of *you*.

By making good choices every day, about what to eat, how much to exercise, and how to handle your problems, *you* can be confident that you are becoming the best you can be.

1
Going from Childhood to Womanhood

Time for a Change

Puberty

Puberty starts with a growth spurt. At least, that's how it appears. It actually starts with a burst of hormones, chemicals that trigger changes in your body. Estrogen is the hormone that's responsible for most of the changes that happen to you at this stage. It makes your breasts develop, hair grow under your arms and around your genitals, and, eventually, your menstrual periods start.

Until estrogen enters your system, there isn't much difference between you and most boys your age. Puberty for boys start with a burst of a different hormone, testosterone. Boys at puberty find their voice getting deeper, their penis getting larger, and hair sprouting on their chest and face.

Before puberty, there is no real difference between the strength and size of boys and girls. But testosterone helps men build muscles. No matter how hard you worked at it, you'd never develop the bulky build you see on some male athletes.

At puberty, men also develop the ability to carry more oxygen in their blood than you can. It means that they can generally outperform women in most sports that require strength and speed.

Your Body Clock

Estrogen is released according to a "body clock" that's set before birth.

No one knows how that clock works — only that it goes off in different girls at different ages. You probably know a few girls your age who seem to be fully developed. At the same time, there may be others who still look like kids. A lot of girls are unhappy about their rate of development; they look at how everyone else is developing and think they're either too "early" or too "late."

Although there are a lot of things you can control as your body goes through puberty, there's nothing you can do to speed up or slow down the clock. The best thing you can do is be prepared for the changes as they come, by knowing what those changes will be and by keeping yourself fit throughout the years when they'll be taking place.

Almost everything about your body begins to change once the estrogen starts to flow. Your bones become longer, thicker, and — with the help of enough calcium in your diet — stronger. You develop reproductive organs and a new layer of fat to protect them. Your skin becomes oily, and you probably start to give off some new odors. The hair under your arms, on your legs, and around your genitals gets thicker and coarser. Your shoulders and hips get wider, and you may shoot up a few inches.

Mixed Emotions

Puberty is very exciting for some girls, and disappointing or even frightening for others.

The excitement comes from watching yourself mature into a woman.

The disappointment may come from finding that your body is turning out to be quite different from what you'd hoped — that you're not going to have the "right" kind of body for gymnastics, for example, or that you're not going to be tall enough to be a model.

The fear may come from being uncomfortable with some of the sexual changes.

Dealing with Disappointment

You can get over your disappointment by becoming familiar with your body. Get to know everything about it. Maybe it has outgrown gymnastics, but can it get pleasure from riding a bike? Swimming? Playing soccer or basketball? How does it react to your moods? Does it slow down when you're sad, or does it get hyper? Does anger give you energy or wear you out? Does happiness make you calm or frantic? And what about food? How do you feel when you eat mostly sweets? What about when you don't eat at all?

Once you've gotten to know how much your body can do for you, and how great it feels when you're taking good care of it, you may forget why you were ever disappointed with it.

Your body is yours, and that's good enough reason to like it. It has limitations, but so does everyone else's.

Forgetting Your Fears

Fears about your sexual development can be hard to deal with, especially if you don't really understand what's happening as you begin to become sexually mature.

Your body is sexually mature when your reproductive organs, breasts, and hormone cycles have developed enough so that you can conceive, carry, deliver, and nurse a baby. Again, your "estrogen clock" determines when this development begins.

Breasts

The first sign that the maturing process has begun appears on your chest, in the form of small
breast "buds." Breasts are also known as mam-
mary glands, glands that produce milk during and
right after pregnancy. But because they are one of
the most obvious changes during puberty, you've
probably found a lot of your friends, and maybe
yourself as well, worrying about when they'll
grow, or whether they'll be "big enough" when
they finally do.

Breast size and the time that breasts take to develop are two more things you can't do anything
about. Maybe you've heard about exercises you
can do or positions you can sleep in to help your
breasts grow faster. The fact is that your body
clock controls the "when." It's hard to say what
controls the "how big," but that's also something
that your body decides on its own. Breast development will take place over several years, so it
may be some time before you know just how large
your breasts will finally be.

Two things can affect your breast development.
If you are overweight, your breasts will carry
some extra padding, too. And if you're underweight, your breasts might not reach their full
size. In other words, if you want to assure yourself that your breasts will be the size that they're
meant to be, don't let yourself get too fat or too
thin.

It's not unusual to feel self-conscious about
your breasts as they're growing, especially if your

friends are always comparing sizes with you and each other, or if boys are making cracks about them all the time. Sometimes the comments boys make (especially if you're one of the first girls in your grade to develop) are embarrassing enough to make you wish your breasts would disappear. Some girls actually try to make that happen, either by hiding themselves under layers of clothing or starving themselves until their breasts shrivel away. Worse, they're apt to remain ashamed of their bodies as adults, and, as a result, never look or feel their best.

If you get teased about your breasts, remind yourself that everyone's body is changing quickly, and soon the breasts of the other girls will catch up to yours or yours will catch up to theirs. Also remember that breasts are a big deal now because they're new, and as soon as everyone has lived with them for a while, the teasing will stop.

But what if it's not just the teasing that bothers you? What if you really don't want breasts? What if you don't understand why everyone else is so anxious to have them?

The idea of becoming an adult, with all of the choices and responsibilities it involves, can be frightening, especially if you're used to having others look after you and protect you. Your developing body reminds you that you will eventually be on your own — and while this can seem exciting, you may not be quite confident enough to feel good about it.

If maturing troubles you, remember that it's a process that takes time. You won't wake up one day to find yourself fully developed, with everyone expecting you to be an adult. It may seem as if all of the changes are happening at once, but you have lots of time to get used to them and help your body adjust. That's what puberty is: the time it takes to become a young woman.

Your Reproductive Organs

Long before you're ready to have children, your body begins preparing for pregnancy. The preparation concerns your reproductive organs, which are located just below your belly button. The same hormones that make your breasts develop, your underarm and pubic hair grow, and your complexion change also affect these organs so that, eventually, you'll be able to give birth.

The organs involved are these:

Vagina: There are three openings to your body between your legs. The first, in front, is the urethra, which you use to urinate. The one in back is your anus, for bowel movements. The middle opening is your vagina. Until puberty you could pretty much ignore your vagina. But soon, if it doesn't already, your menstrual flow will pass through it. And if you decide to use tampons during your periods, this is where you'll insert them. (More about tampons on page 192.) A baby passes out of its mother's body through the mother's vagina.

Cervix: The passageway between your vagina and

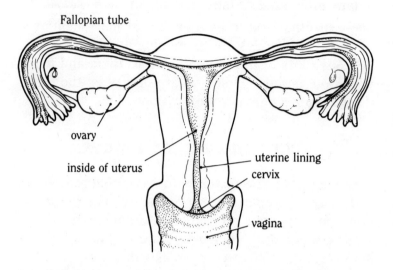

Fallopian tube

ovary

inside of uterus

uterine lining

cervix

vagina

your uterus is your cervix. During puberty the wall of your cervix begins to produce a clear, sticky mucus. That mucus will be part of your menstrual flow. During pregnancy it keeps dangerous bacteria out of the mother's uterus.

Uterus, or womb: This is where the baby would develop if you were to get pregnant. The walls of your uterus are incredibly stretchy, able to expand enough to hold an infant, twins, or maybe even quintuplets.

Ovaries: One ovary sits on each side of your uterus. No bigger than a walnut, each ovary contains hundreds of thousands of "follicles," microscopic sacs containing even more microscopic "eggs." Each egg is called an ovum, and if fertilized by a sperm cell it would begin to develop into a baby.

Fallopian Tubes: Hanging down from each side of your uterus and reaching out toward your ovaries, the Fallopian tubes are like tunnels for an ovum to pass through on its way to your uterus. Each month, once your periods begin, one ovum will burst out of its follicle and enter a Fallopian tube. Fine hairs along the tube help push the ovum along toward the uterus.

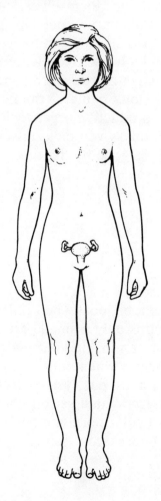

Changes on the Outside ___ *That Match Changes Within* ___

Each of these organs has been part of your body since birth, but they start to function only after you reach puberty. Their function, basically, is to enable you to have children. You can't see the changes in the organs themselves, but you can tell that they're taking place. Your hips get wider — this is so there would be room for your uterus to stretch and hold a baby if you were to get pregnant. Also, you get a little extra padding around your stomach. Don't panic — the fat is there to protect your reproductive organs while they're developing. And unless you pick up some poor eating habits, it'll be gone by the time you're fully developed.

Menstruation

It seems like a big deal when it first happens, but your period is only a small part of the chain of events that goes on inside your body each month.

The chain begins when your brain sends a large hormone spurt into your system. Remember, hormones are "triggers" that set off changes in your body. This particular hormone lands in your ovaries, where it douses your follicles.

One of the follicles begins to manufacture a hormone of its own: estrogen. The estrogen seeps into your uterus. Once there, the estrogen helps to create a thick lining for the wall of the uterus.

Next, another hormone hits the follicle, forcing it to break open. An egg pops out and gets swept up into one of your Fallopian tubes.

Once the egg is gone, the follicle turns yellow and begins to produce yet another hormone. This hormone is called progesterone, and it, too, goes into your uterus. Like estrogen, it helps thicken the wall of your uterus.

Meanwhile, the ovum is traveling through the Fallopian tube on its way to your uterus. If a woman has sexual intercourse while the egg is making the trip, there's a good chance that a sperm cell will meet up with it and fertilize it. When a woman is carrying a fertilized egg, she is pregnant.

The fertilized egg reaches the uterus, which by now has a soft, sturdy lining, thanks to the estrogen and progesterone that were working away in there. The lining provides nutrients as well as protection for the egg, which over the course of nine months will turn into a full-fledged baby.

But if the egg does not get fertilized by the time it reaches the uterus (and most of them never will), the hormones taper off. Since there's no fertilized egg for the lining to nourish and protect, you don't need it anymore.

Your body's functioning to get rid of the lining from your uterus is called menstruation. **Pregnant** women don't menstruate, because the lining is needed to feed and cushion the baby.

What You're Really Losing Each Month

Even though it can look very bloody (and — at least the first time — scary), only about half of your menstrual fluid is blood. The rest is mucus, worn-out cells, and other bits of the lining from the uterus. All of those other things are clear, but the blood stains them red, making it look like the entire flow is blood.

You should get into the habit of writing down the first day of each period. It'll help you keep track of when your next one is due, and will also come in handy at your next doctor's appointment. Your next period should come roughly twenty-eight days after the previous one started. But everyone's body runs on a different schedule. Some girls get their period exactly four weeks apart; others have three or five weeks in between. Sometimes you may get one period four weeks after another, and then wait two months for the next one. Hardly anyone is absolutely regular all of the time, but you should check with your doctor if you're worried about your menstruation pattern.

Why You May Not Have Started Menstruating Yet _____ (Even If Your Friends Have) _____

Body Clock

The most likely reason that you're "behind" your friends is that your body clock is set to go off a year or two after theirs.

You can pretty much tell when your first period will come. It usually starts two to three years after the first signs of breasts appear on your chest. Those breast buds let you know that the hormones have started cranking up. And once that process begins, your periods will follow. For most girls, this occurs between the ages of eleven and fourteen. Still, it's not unusual for periods to start in girls as young as ten or as old as seventeen.

Not Enough Fat

Another reason you may not have begun to menstruate is that you are thinner or more muscular than your friends. You must have a certain amount of fat protecting your body before your periods will start. Doctors really don't know how much fat — and they certainly don't mean that you should *be* fat — but they know that you can't be all muscle or bone.

Your doctor can probably tell you if you're underweight, but he or she won't be able to say for sure if that's the reason your periods haven't started yet. Even so, your doctor will suggest that you get your weight up to where it should be, so that you'll have a better chance of functioning normally in every way.

As for being too muscular, it's almost impossible to tell if this is why you're not menstruating yet, and it's not really worth quitting your exercise program to find out. Eventually your body should turn some of the muscle into just enough fat for your periods to start.

Too Much Exercise

While exercise can help you have regular, pain-free periods, overdoing it can keep you from having any periods at all. The hormones that your body produces while you're working out can get in the way of the hormones you need for menstruation.

Many young athletes know that tough training can stop their menstrual cycles. Some of them interpret having a period to mean that they're not training hard enough, and they begin to train harder, hoping to make them stop. This is definitely a dangerous idea.

The fact is that not having periods works against you in a number of ways. First of all, the hormones that help produce your periods also help to build and strengthen your bones. Your period is a sign that your body has enough of that hormone to make your bones strong. Not having periods may mean that your body doesn't.

Second, that hormone is important to your heart. Some women begin to have heart trouble when they go without it for long. In other words, you lose some of the very benefits of exercise — strong bones and a healthy heart — if you overdo it enough to disrupt menstruation.

See the section on movement (starting on page 101) to plan a safe, effective exercise routine.

Poor Nourishment

A lot of nutrients go into preparing your body to menstruate, and unless you get all that you need, your periods won't begin. The section on nutrition (starting on page 33) will help you tell if you're eating the right foods, as well as suggest ways to improve your diet so that your periods, and your body in general, will be as they should.

What Sexual Maturity Means

Once your periods start, you're able to get pregnant. Until you're ready to care for and support a baby, you should know how to keep yourself from having one.

Only One Way to Get Pregnant; One Way to Avoid It

Having sexual intercourse is the only way to get pregnant. And the only guaranteed way to make sure you won't get pregnant is to avoid sexual intercourse. Even the first time — just as much as any time — pregnancy is a big risk.

Pregnancy isn't the only risk; you may end up (as millions of people have) with a sexually transmitted disease (a type of disease passed only through sexual activity). Sexually transmitted diseases can cause anything from painful sores inside your vagina to brain damage and death.

Healthy Thoughts about Sex

Adults may tell you that you're too young to be thinking about sex, anyway. But there's no way you can help it. For one thing, your period and developing shape remind you that your body is becoming more sexual. For another, almost every television show, movie, and rock video involves sex in some way — usually in a way that gives no clue to the amount of responsibility involved in a sexual relationship or in protecting yourself from pregnancy and sexually transmitted disease.

Those shows, movies, and videos make sex seem as if it's the only thing that matters in a relationship. Although sex can be a powerful, vital expression of love, there must be tremendous trust and caring in a relationship before it can bring the pleasure you've heard about. The emphasis on sex in magazines, music, movies, and so forth may make you feel left out if you haven't experienced sex yet. But keep in mind that while some girls your age may like one or two boys a lot, most don't feel close enough to anyone to take the risks that sexual intercourse involves.

When Your Friends
Start Talking . . .

about how "far they've gone," remember that a lot of girls use sex to get attention. They think it's the only way they can get guys to care about them and make other girls admire them. Some of them may not enjoy having sex, but lack the confidence to try to develop friendships in other ways. So, even if sex makes them uncomfortable, they keep doing it as long as the attention lasts.

It usually doesn't last long, though. Most of those girls become lonely when they discover that it's easier to get a boy to mess around with them than to be the kind of friend they really need.

Some girls fall for the idea that sex will make them cool or that it will turn them into "women" overnight. It never works out that way. In fact, a lot of girls end up feeling worse — and less positive about themselves — when they discover that sex doesn't solve all of their problems.

Having sex doesn't make you into a woman any more than wearing makeup and high heels does. Being a woman involves taking responsibility for your health and your feelings. One way to do that is to realize that sex, although wonderful when it's an appropriate part of a loving relationship with strong trust and caring, involves serious responsibility.

Lots of girls have learned this the hard way — by getting pregnant. Many of them got pregnant because they just didn't believe it could happen to them. Obviously, they were wrong.

Pregnancy Would Change Your Life

And probably not for the better. For most girls it means dropping out of school, getting a boring job, and losing their boyfriend. Studies prove that most teenage boys who get a girlfriend pregnant leave her either before or right after the baby is born — even if they promised to marry or care for her.

Pregnancy can also ruin your health. There can be nothing worse for a growing body like yours than to have another body growing inside it. Your body needs lots of nourishment as it's developing, and a developing baby needs even more. It's nearly impossible to provide enough nutrients for both of you to grow fully and normally. For that reason, many pregnant teenagers have babies with brain damage and other birth defects.

A Sexually Transmitted Disease (STD) Can Ruin Your Health, and More

So far, there is no cure for herpes, the most common STD. You get herpes, and all STDs, by having sexual intercourse with someone who has it. Herpes shows up as itchy, burning sores inside your vagina that may come and go throughout your life. Babies born to mothers with herpes often have brain damage and/or the disease themselves.

There is also no cure for AIDS, an STD that is always fatal. While most AIDS victims in America are either men who have had sex with men carrying the AIDS virus, or drug users who have injected themselves with contaminated needles, women do get AIDS from sex with infected men.

Other STDs, like syphilis and gonorrhea, can leave you unable to have children when you're ready for them. Chlamydia, a vaginal infection you can pick up during intercourse, may spread to your ovaries and ruin your chances to have children as well.

Even those STDs that are impossible to cure are easy to prevent: if you don't have sex, you won't get AIDS or any other STD.

Avoiding STDs is another reason to put off having sex until you're in a close, trusting relationship. Only someone who genuinely loves you will do what's needed to avoid spreading an STD, including telling you if he has one, not having sex with anyone else, and using a condom.

Saying No to Sex

If someone tells you that he'll like you better if you have sex with him, or that your relationship will improve if you start sleeping together, he's lying. One way to respond to pressure like that is to say, "If you care about me enough to want to have sex with me, then you should care enough to understand why I don't want to do it, and stop trying to make me do something I don't want to do."

It's important to keep yourself from being coerced (sweet-talked, teased) into having sex. Only you can know when you feel enough trust, caring, and love to share yourself in that way. Pushing yourself before you're ready can cause emotional and physical discomfort — even pain. A bad experience now could prevent you from enjoying close, pleasurable sexual relationships at an appropriate time later in life.

Where to Go for Information about Sex

Your Mother

If she hasn't brought it up yet, it may be because she's waiting for the "right" time, or because she's intimidated by it. As soon as you mention it, she'll know that the time is right. Not everyone is comfortable talking about sex, so you might have a tough time getting a discussion started. But once you have, you'll feel better about bringing it up any time you want.

Your Doctor

Your doctor may ask you if you want information about birth control, but that doesn't mean that he or she expects you to be having sexual intercourse. He or she wants to make absolutely sure you have some reliable protection just in case you need it. If your doctor doesn't mention birth control, ask about it. It's a good way to learn how your reproductive system works and how careful you'll have to be with it throughout your life.

Planned Parenthood

This organization is dedicated to helping girls and women avoid having unwanted pregnancies. You'll find the local branch listed in the white pages phone directory, and you can call them to set up an appointment to discuss sex and birth control with one of their counselors. Bring a friend along so that the next time you and she share information about sex, you'll both really know what you're talking about.

Where Not *to Go for Information about Sex*

Even though some of your friends may actually know something about sex, they can be the source of *wrong* information, like "You can't get pregnant your first time" (you can, and many girls do),

"You won't get pregnant if you douche right after" (you can), and so on. That kind of wrong information can be very dangerous. It's better to talk with supportive adults, like your parents, your doctor, or planned parenthood counselors, who are better equipped to advise you.

Your Body, Your Rules: Recognizing and Stopping Sexual Abuse

All of your life people have been making rules for you: when to go to bed, when to turn in your homework, what to wear to school, and so forth. But there is at least one rule that you can make for everyone else, and which everyone else has to obey. That rule is: "Nobody, but *nobody*, can touch my body unless I let them. No one in my family has this right. None of my friends has this right. My teachers, neighbors, coaches, parents' friends — none of them has this right."

No one claims to understand fully why some adults force, trick, or bribe young girls into touching them in sexual ways or having sex with them. It's becoming common knowledge that it happens a lot and that it's always wrong, it's always the adult's fault, and it's always against the law.

_____ *What Is Sexual Abuse?* _____

Sexual abuse often involves touching, but it doesn't have to. Sexual abuse includes being asked or made to:

○ look at someone's penis
○ undress so someone can see you naked
○ look at pictures of naked children or adults
○ pose naked for photographs
○ have someone touch your breasts, vagina, or buttocks
○ touch someone's penis
○ have sexual intercourse with someone

Most girls who are victims of sexual abuse are too scared, embarrassed, or confused to stop it when it happens or to prevent it from happening again. If you're one of them, it may be because the adult has said something like:

○ "We'll *both* get into trouble."
○ "I'll hurt you or take away your privileges."
○ "I'd have to go to jail, and it would be your fault; everyone would hate you."
○ "It's my way of showing you that I love you, but no one else would understand that."
○ "This is something very special between us. Your mother would be so jealous she might kill herself or do something to hurt you."
○ "What do you think fathers (or uncles, older friends, or older brothers) are for? To teach

you how to do this so you'll be ready when you're grown up!"

No matter what he says to try to make it seem as if what he's doing is okay, and no matter what he tells you to try to make you think that things would be worse if you told someone and forced him to stop, he is *wrong*. He is using you, and he's just saying those things so he can keep getting his way. He knows you don't want to go along with him, so he makes up reasons to get you to do it. He doesn't care how you feel, and he doesn't really care about what happens to your family. If he did, he never would have started abusing you in the first place.

Reporting Abuse

It's time to report it. You can:

○ call the police directly and tell them you want to report that you are an abused minor
○ call the Child Abuse Hotline, listed in the "Community Services" section at the front of the white pages phone directory
○ call the Rape Crisis Center, also listed in the "Community Services" section at the front of the white pages phone directory
○ talk to your favorite teacher and ask her to make the call for you
○ talk to your best friend's mother, and ask her to make the call for you

Keep these things in mind when you call or ask for help: "I am a victim. He (whoever he is) is wrong. As a victim, I deserve protection, and somebody will want to help me."

What about Your Mother?

If it's your father, your mother's boyfriend, or someone else close to your mother who's been touching you, then your mother would be a very heroic person if she could stand up to the news without being very upset and hurt, especially if he's someone she loves. She may be confused for a while, and get angry at you instead of at the man involved. Things will probably be easier for both of you if you don't tell your mother until after you've contacted the police and talked with an understanding adult who will support and help you. They will make sure that she has someone to help her deal with her feelings, and that there will be someone to do the same for you.

You will be asked to tell what's happened to you over and over again. Sometimes you'll get the feeling that they want you to change your story. Don't. Stick with the truth, and don't let anyone try to convince you that you really weren't bothered by what he did to you. Don't let anyone get away with suggesting that it wasn't a big deal. It was, and is, and you deserve the very best treatment and protection now that you've let others know about it.

2
Nourishment

If you're like a lot of people, you think about food
only when you're hungry or bored, and then all
that matters to you is filling your stomach with
something tasty.

But food deserves more consideration than that,
especially now. The way your body will turn out
has a lot to do with what you put into it while
you're growing. If you want bones that are sturdy
enough to hold you up and keep you together, the
time to eat the kinds of foods that will make them
strong is *now* — while your bones are still form-
ing.

If you want to be free of weight problems and
heart trouble, the time to avoid foods that contain
lots of fat is *now* — while your habits and cells are
still taking shape. And if you care about your
complexion, now is the time to make sure that you
eat enough vitamins and protein to protect and
nourish your skin.

It is also the time to stay off weight-loss diets
(unless your doctor puts you on one). Growing

and maturing take more nourishment than you've ever needed before. Dieting can be dangerous because it usually means leaving out many foods that your body needs to make the change from kid to adult.

What Is Food?

Even though it's easy to recognize when it's on your plate, it's hard to say what food really is. Food would not be food unless it provided energy and nutrients. Energy is what keeps you going. Nutrients build your body and allow it to function. Each nutrient has at least one specific job, and no nutrient can cover for any of the others. Because you need many different nutrients to stay healthy, you have to eat a wide variety of foods in order to get all of them. If you stick to just one or two favorite foods (even healthy foods like cottage cheese or fruit), you'll run short of the nutrients you must have to stay well.

Foods without nutrients are known as *junk*. Junk also includes foods with ingredients that can actually harm you. Eating junk when you're trying to look and feel your best is like throwing trash on the floor when you're trying to keep your room clean. It just works against you.

To get the most from this chapter, begin with the chart on the next page. Follow the directions, keeping track of what you eat for three days. Later in the chapter, the charts will help you compare what you have been eating with what you should be eating.

Four for You

As you can see from the way the chart is set up, every serving you're supposed to have during the day comes from one of four different food groups. Foods fall into groups according to what they do for your body, and each group has specific responsibilities that none of the other groups can handle. If you don't eat enough from the vegetable group, for example, you _can't_ make up for it by eating twice as much from the bread group. Here's why:

Bread, Grains, and Cereals: This group provides energy for your body and mind. Without it, you'd be weak, grouchy, and unable to think straight.

Meat, Fish, and Legumes: This group provides protein. Without it, you wouldn't grow. Your hair would fall out, and your nails would chip.

Milk and Cheeses: This group provides the mineral calcium. Without it, your bones would rot and your teeth would fall out. The tiny bones along your spine would break, so that you'd have a humped back.

Fruits and Vegetables: This group provides vitamins, especially vitamins A and C. Without it, your gums would bleed, your skin would get scaly, and your eyes wouldn't work in the dark.

What Are You Eating?

Use this chart to keep track of everything you eat for three days. (It'll be easiest to use if you make three copies and use a different one each day). Whenever you eat something, put a check (✔) next to it. If the food isn't listed here, write it in under the group where it belongs. Be sure to include everything you have during the day — snacks and candy, too.

Breads, Grains, and Cereals

You need no less than four servings and no more than six each day. (Each item listed represents one serving.)

- □ bread: 2 thin slices or 1 thick slice; 1 small bagel, or ½ large; 1 small roll or ½ large
- □ crackers: 4 to 8, depending on size
- □ rice: 1 cup, cooked
- □ pasta (spaghetti, macaroni, noodles): 1 cup, cooked
- □ breakfast cereal (hot or cold): ¼ cup to 1 cup — check package label for serving size
- □ tortillas: 2 small or 1 large

Meat, Fish, and Legumes

(Legumes are beans like kidney, pinto, navy, soy, or garbanzo beans.) You need no less than two servings and no more than four each day.

- □ beef: 3 ounces
- □ pork: 3 ounces
- □ lamb: 3 ounces
- □ liver: 3 ounces
- □ chicken: 3 ounces
- □ turkey: 3 ounces
- □ fish: 3 ounces
- □ egg: 1
- □ beans or lentils: 1 cup, cooked
- □ peanut butter: 2 tablespoons
- □ tofu: 7 ounces

Milk and Cheeses

You need no less than four and no more than six servings each day.

- □ milk: 1 cup
- □ yogurt: 1 cup
- □ cheese (except cream cheese and cottage cheese): 1 ounce
- □ cottage cheese: ½ cup

Fruits and Vegetables

You need at least four servings, including one citrus fruit and one dark green vegetable each day.
Important: Serving sizes given here are for *fresh* fruits and vegetables. Sizes for foods that are canned or frozen in sauces or syrup will be different.

- □ broccoli: 1 large stalk
- □ spinach: ½ cup
- □ Brussels sprouts: ½ cup
- □ kale: ½ cup
- □ okra: ½ cup
- □ asparagus: 4 stalks

Milk and Cheeses	Fruits and Vegetables
	☐ collard greens: ½ cup ☐ orange (or juice): 1 orange or 1 cup juice ☐ grapefruit (or juice): 1 grapefruit or 1 cup juice ☐ tomato (or juice): 1 tomato or 1 cup juice ☐ apple (or juice): 1 apple or 1 cup juice ☐ pear: 1 ☐ peach/nectarine: 1 ☐ strawberries: ½ cup ☐ grapes: ½ cup ☐ cauliflower: ½ cup ☐ potato: 2 small or 1 baking size ☐ corn: 1 ear or 1 cup kernels
Extras	
Here's where to list the foods you have during the day that *don't* fall into one of the groups above. Candy, soda, doughnuts, butter or margarine, or potato chips, for example, belong right here.	

You might wonder where pizza fits in, or tacos, or macaroni and cheese. It's not hard to figure out.

If you learn what goes into various foods, you'll know which food groups they include. Pizza, for example, contains crust (bread group), cheese (milk group), and tomato sauce (fruit and vegetable group). Tacos contain a shell (bread group), meat filling (meat group), and cheese (milk group). Add lettuce and tomato, and you're including the fruit and vegetable group, too. Macaroni and cheese contains pasta (bread group) and cheese (milk group).

Calories

The energy in food is called calories. Everyone talks about them as if they're the last things you'd want to put into your body. But the truth is, you need them. More people in the world die from too few calories than from too many. You need them because your body's always using energy, whether you're running, walking, or standing still. Cut back on calories too much, and your system will slow down. Lay off them altogether, and you'll die.

Calories:

○ supply energy for growth
○ provide energy so that your heart, lungs,

brain, and other organs can operate to keep you alive
- give you energy for being physically active
- give you energy for thinking

If calories are so great, why is everyone so paranoid about them?

Because it's far too easy to get too many of them, and extra calories turn into fat. You get fat if you take in more calories than your body can use. To avoid getting fat, you have to eat as many calories as you need, and no more. Some people manage that by figuring out how many calories they use in a day, memorizing the amount in various foods, then adding them up as they chew and swallow.

But counting calories can make mealtime more tedious than math class. Unless your doctor has put you on a special weight-loss diet, you don't have to bring your calculator to the dinner table. Just having a general idea about how many calories are in the foods you eat should be enough to help you keep excess calories from becoming excess fat.

A Calorie Is a Calorie Is a Calorie

An important point to remember is that all calories are the same. The calories in a piece of strawberry shortcake are not more fattening than the calories in a strawberry. The shortcake is more fattening than the strawberry because it contains *more* calories, not a different kind of calories. In other words, foods vary greatly in the number of calories they give you, so it's not only the amount you eat that matters, but the number of calories in the food you choose to eat. You could, for example, eat one piece of strawberry shortcake and end up consuming many more calories than you'd get from eating several baskets of plain, fresh strawberries.

There are a lot of overweight people around who complain that they get fat even though they don't eat much. Well, maybe they're not eating big meals, but the foods they eat at those meals are probably very high in calories.

Remember:

○ Growing bodies need more calories than grown ones. That's one reason why you shouldn't put yourself on a low-calorie diet right now, without checking with your doctor. If you just start hacking away at the calories in your diet, chances are good that you'll disturb your growth in some way.
○ Busy bodies need more than lazy ones. When you're active you spend energy that could be helping you grow. You have to make up for it by eating more.
○ Large bodies need more energy than small ones. The more body you have, the more energy it takes to keep it going.

How can you tell how many calories are in the foods you eat?

One way is to know how much fat is in the food. Fat has more calories than any other nutrient, and any food that contains lots of fat is loaded with calories.

The easiest way to tell how many calories are in a particular food is to read the nutrition information label on the package it comes in. At the top of the label, it says *nutrition information per serving*. Just below that, it says *serving size,* and gives you a measurement. The serving size may be 1 cup, ½ cup, ¼ cup, 8 ounces, 6 ounces. It varies. Below that it says how many servings the package contains. Then it tells you how many calories are in one serving.

So, if a package of cereal says that a serving size is 1 cup, and tells you there are 100 calories in one serving, then you know there are 100 calories in 1 cup of cereal. If you're going to pour milk on your cereal, look for the number of calories per serving on the milk carton. Add that number to the 100 calories for the cereal. Now you'll know exactly how many calories are in your bowl.

You can use the nutrition information labels to compare the number of calories in different brands and types of foods.

Nutrients

Nutrients make the difference between real food and junk food. You could say it's like the difference between practical clothes and clothes you'd

Read the Label

This label is telling you how many nutrients are in one *serving*, not one package. If you eat this much, you'll get exactly the number of calories and nutrients listed here. If you eat half this amount, you'll get half of everything on the list. Remember, this is a measuring cup, not to be confused with any other kind.

This is how many servings this package contains — if the servings you eat are the same size as the "serving size" listed above. This package contains eight servings, if each serving is 1 cup.

This is how many calories are in one serving, when that serving is the same size as the "serving size." There are 90 calories in one serving of this — if your serving is 1 cup. If your serving is larger, it will have more calories. If it's smaller, it'll have fewer.

Nutrition Information per Serving:

Serving Size   1 cup
Servings per Container   8
Calories   90
Protein   9 grams
Carbohydrate   12 grams
Fat   0 grams

Ingredients:

Here's where you look to find out exactly what's in the food in this package. Ingredients are always listed from most to least. If wheat flour is the first ingredient, the product contains more flour than anything else. If sugar is first, then it's mostly sugar.

wear just for fun. A diet of ice cream and chips would be as good for fueling your body as a wardrobe of lacy dresses would be for wearing to school.

There are six types of nutrients.

1. Protein
2. Carbohydrates
3. Fat
4. Vitamins
5. Minerals
6. Water

Protein

The main reason you need protein is that it's what you're made of. No protein, no you. Your body can't make protein on its own, so your life depends on getting it from the foods you eat. Fortunately, protein is easy to come by.

Protein:

○ keeps you growing and developing; the cells that make up your body can't build and reproduce without it
○ helps you fight off infections and recover from injuries and disease
○ keeps your muscles firm
○ makes your nails sturdy and your hair healthy
○ gives you emergency energy in case you haven't eaten enough carbohydrates

What Is Junk and What Is Food?

This chart demonstrates the difference between real food and junk.

Food/Serving Size	Calories	Any Nutrients?	What's in It for You
skim (nonfat) milk, 1 cup	90	protein, carbohydrate, calcium, vitamins A, B₂, and D	strong teeth and bones; normal growth and development; clear, bright eyes
Compare It with			
McDonald's chocolate shake, 1	360	carbohydrate, fat, some calcium	fast-burning energy (in other words, energy that doesn't last long)
lowfat vanilla yogurt, 1 container	200	protein, carbohydrate, calcium, vitamins A, B₂, and D	same as milk, plus fast-burning energy
Compare It with			
vanilla ice cream, 1 cup	350	carbohydrate, fat, some calcium but not enough to count	same as the milkshake above
turkey sandwich on whole wheat bread	240 (aprox.)	protein, carbohydrate, B vitamins, fiber	lasting energy, healthy skin and hair
Compare It with			
hot dog on a bun	280	carbohydrate, fat, some protein but not enough to compete with turkey, chicken, tuna, or a lean	fat, fat, and more fat, plus you'll get thirsty from all the salt

	no butter, sour cream, or cheese added)		and possibly some forms of cancer; healthy gums and skin
Compare It with			
french fries, 1 order at McDonald's	220	vitamin C; some of the same vitamins as a baked potato, although many of them are destroyed by the heat of the fryer; sodium	possibly dangerous high blood pressure from the salt; excess fat

Protein does some amazing things, but there are lots of myths around that make it seem more incredible than it is. One is the myth that protein builds muscle. It doesn't. The protein in your system *supports* the muscle, holding it firm. But you have to work at *developing* that muscle; protein can't do that for you. An athlete who thinks she needs a lot of protein should know that she doesn't need any more than anyone else her size. In fact, too much protein actually makes you weaker; it tends to make muscles store water, which weighs them down.

Another myth about protein is that high-protein foods are less fattening than other foods. You may have heard this from a dieter who'd rather eat the burger and leave the bun.

In fact, pure protein has exactly as many calories as pure carbohydrates. But most foods that are high in protein are also high in fat, while most carbohydrates don't contain any fat (unless you add it by buttering your bread, heaping sour cream on your potato, or pouring cream on your cereal, for example). Since fat has twice as many calories as protein alone, protein foods containing fat (that includes burgers) have many more calories than plain bread, potatoes, and other carbohydrates.

There are lean (fat-free) protein foods, and they usually have more nutrients and fewer calories than the fatty ones. They include fish, various types of beans, and skim dairy products. Those are the sources you should choose if you're concerned about your weight.

Another myth about protein is that you have to

eat meat in order to get it. Adults are apt to use this tactic to get you to eat something you think is disgusting, like meat loaf. Kids use it sometimes, too, to justify eating burgers at least once a day.

The fact is, you can get protein that's as good as what you'd get from meat by combining beans, nuts, eggs, or cheese with bread, rice, pasta, or corn.

Finally, there is no truth to the myth that extra protein makes you extra energetic. Too little protein makes you weak. But extra protein — like extra anything — only makes you fat. On the chart below, you'll see how easy it is to get all of the protein you need in a day.

If you can't get 46 grams of protein from what you've been eating each day, look for ways to substitute good protein sources for foods that contain little or none of it. For example, have a tuna sandwich (24 grams of protein) instead of a hot dog (7 grams). Or have a few slices of turkey (27 grams) instead of a BLT (4 grams).

If you happen to come out with much more than 46, you can think about cutting out some of the protein-rich foods you've been eating and adding foods that supply some other nutrient you may be short on (like iron, calcium, or various vitamins). For example, instead of having an egg for breakfast, you might have a bowl of iron-fortified cereal with a cup of milk. That way you'd be exchanging excess protein for needed iron and calcium. Or you could have a salad of fresh vegetables, cheese, and garbanzo beans instead of a ham sandwich for lunch. You'd still get some protein,

Can You Make Your Protein Add Up?
(You need 46 grams each day.)

Look back over your three-day eating chart and write down all the sources of protein. Then find their values in the list below, and add them up. If you come out with 46 grams or more each day, you can be sure that you're getting as much protein as you need.
Check for:

bacon, 2 slices: 3.8 g
hot dog, 1 (2 ounces): 7 g
hamburger, McDonald's Big Mac,
    Burger King Whopper: 26 g
pizza, ¼ 14-inch pie: 15.6 g
turkey, white meat (3 ounces): 27 g
tuna packed in water (3 ounces): 24 g
tuna packed in oil (3 ounces): 47 g
milk, skim (1 cup): 9 g
milk, whole (1 cup): 8 g
peanut butter (2 tablespoons): 8 g
egg, 1 large: 7 g
cheddar cheese (1 ounce): 8 g
yogurt (1 cup): 8 g
beans (1 cup cooked): 22 g
pork sausage (2 links): 5 g

but you'd replace extra protein with iron, vitamins, and calcium.

Carbohydrates

Unless you're on some whacky (and dangerous) diet, you eat more carbohydrates than anything else — because more foods *are* carbohydrates than anything else. Potatoes, pasta, bread, rice, fruits of all kinds, honey, and sugar — all are carbohydrates. What makes carbohydrates alike, obviously, is not the way they taste, but the fact that they're made of sugar. Sugar takes different forms, so that the sugar in a potato or a string of spaghetti tastes different from the sugar you'd find in a candy bar or in a can of soda. The different forms of sugar not only have different flavors, but, more important, have different effects on you.

Carbohydrates have gotten a really bad break from people who think they're fattening. The truth is that most carbohydrates contain no fat at all. Plain potatoes, rice, pasta, and many types of bread are fat-free. The fat comes along with the butter, cream, and cheese that you add to them.

Carbohydrates:

○ Give you energy. Of all the nutrients, carbohydrates are the best source of energy. It takes a while for the energy from protein and fat to get into your system. Your body can use the energy from carbohydrates right away.

○ Provide vitamins. Most carbohydrates contain lots of vitamins.

○ Contain fiber. Fiber is the rough stuff in food

that keeps your digestive system "regular." In other words, it helps you avoid the discomfort and pain that can result from going for several days without a bowel movement.

But not all carbohydrates provide these benefits. Plain sugar, honey, syrup, and molasses don't add anything to your diet but flavor and calories. In fact, they actually make you hungrier and weaker than before you ate them. Here's what happens:

1. You're hungry.
2. You eat a candy bar.
3. You're not hungry anymore, because the sugar from the candy is immediately released in your blood, which carries the energy from the sugar to your brain. When your brain is receiving energy, you don't feel hungry.
4. But now your body reacts. It can't handle that much sugar. It produces a substance called insulin to clear the sugar out of your blood.
5. The insulin does what it's supposed to do — and more. It gets rid of the sugar from the candy, plus whatever sugar was left in your body from an earlier meal.
6. There's no sugar left to provide energy for your body or your brain. You feel hungry again. And then the cycle begins all over.

If you're going to have lasting energy, you have to eat foods that release their sugar slowly. Carbohydrates that have less "obvious" sugar (carbohydrates that don't taste really sweet) give you the kind of energy that lasts. So bread, crackers, and unsweetened cereals make much better snacks than candy, cookies, cakes, or ice cream.

The best carbohydrates are fresh fruits, vegetables, whole grain breads, cereals, crackers, and pasta. They carry lots of vitamins and fiber, and they release sugar slowly, providing energy that lasts a long time.

Comparing Carbohydrates	
Excellent	Diabolical
whole wheat bread	sweet rolls
English muffins	doughnuts*
brown rice	stuffing mix*
whole grain, enriched cereal	sweetened cereal
baked potatoes	french fries*
fresh, steamed vegetables	potato chips*
	frozen vegetables
	in cream sauce*
whole wheat crackers	saltines*
	cookies
	*High in fat.

Fat

The good news about fat is that you should eat some.

The bad news is that you'll probably eat as much as you need even if you never have another ice cream cone, french fry, or doughnut. The amount of fat you need is so small that you couldn't ever legitimately claim that you need cheesecake to avoid a dietary deficiency. You get plenty from the meat, cheese, eggs, and other nutritious foods that you normally eat.

Fat:

○ Keeps your system cool in summer and warm in winter.

○ Makes your skin and hair look and feel "alive." People who don't eat enough generally have crummy skin and brittle hair.

○ Protects your bones and your organs. Imagine how it would feel to sit down without a layer of fat back there to cushion you.

○ Helps your body use some essential vitamins. Vitamins A, D, E, and K won't work without fat.

You don't have to eat fatty foods to get fat. You get fat by eating too much, no matter what it is. It happens to be easier to eat too much fat, because straight fat has twice as many calories as protein and carbohydrates. To make things worse, those calories don't come along with any nutrients, as the calories from protein and carbohydrates usually do.

Worse still, your body has a tough time using the energy from fat, so it's more likely to get stored away than the energy from other foods. And stored energy means fat.

The ugly side of fat, obvously, is what shows.

But what doesn't show is just as bad. That's the damage it can do to your heart. Fat is heavy, and whenever you lug around extra weight, your heart has to work harder. If you get overweight and stay that way long enough, you'll wear out your heart before its time. Avoiding fatty foods today is one sure way of protecting yourself for the future.

Fat Cells Are Forever

There are only two times during your life when you can add fat cells to your body. Infancy was one of them. Now is the other. The fewer fat cells you have by the time you stop growing, the harder it will be for your body to collect fat. The more fat cells you have, the harder it will be to get rid of fat. Clearly, now is the time to start avoiding fats. Watch it now, and you won't be stuck forever with a body full of fat-hoarding cells.

Fat can creep into your diet in all sorts of ways, adding fat cells and extra calories, and taking the place of more important nutrients. See page 54 for some ways you can keep that from happening.

Two Types of Fat

Even though all fats have the same number of calories (margarine, for example, has just as many as salad oil, butter, and lard), some fats are less harmful to your body than others. What makes some worse than others is the fact that they con-

Fat-Fighting Tips

* Cut away any fat that you see on your meat before you put it into your mouth. Peel the skin off chicken; there'll hardly be any fat left.

* Whenever you cook, spray your pans with "no stick" spray instead of coating them with oil or butter. Get whoever else does the cooking in your house to do the same thing.

* If you eat peanut butter, make sure it's the kind that's made from peanuts only. Lots of brands contain added oil, which means they have unnecessary fat and calories.

* Whenever you make scrambled eggs, use one whole egg and just the white from another. Your eggs will be fluffy, and they'll have half the fat and nearly half the calories of two whole eggs. Also, you'll get twice as much protein as you would from one egg, since egg white is nearly pure protein.

tain *cholesterol*. Once it's in your body, cholesterol is like a wax, traveling through your bloodstream. Eventually it can build up into a hard ball, blocking your arteries so blood can't get through. If that happened, you'd have a heart attack or a stroke (a stroke can cause part of your brain to die from lack of blood).

Cholesterol starts building up in your blood while you're a kid, and keeps accumulating as you grow, unless you learn how to eat to avoid it. One way is to limit the number of eggs you eat each week to two or three. Egg yolks are loaded with cholesterol. Another way is to watch out for saturated fats, the kind of fat that comes from animals. Saturated fats nearly always raise your cholesterol.

Saturated fats are found in:

> butter
> lard
> cheeses
> whole milk
> ice cream
> cream
> meat, bacon, sausage

Fats that come from vegetables and most fish don't add cholesterol to your system. In fact, some actually help to get rid of what might already be there. Vegetable fats are called *polyunsaturated fats*.

Even though it's not good to have much of any kind of fat, you're better off eating foods that contain polyunsatuated fats.

Polyunsaturated fats are found in:

> corn oil
> safflower oil
> vegetable oil

Vitamins

Around the turn of the century, some laboratory rats were fed pure protein, carbohydrate, and fat, the only nutrients known at the time. The rats died because something was missing from their diet. That something was vitamins.

Vitamins:

○ help your body use the energy from the food you eat
○ help manufacture blood
○ release nutrients from foods and help your body use them; no matter how much protein you eat, for example, it won't do you any good unless you also eat the vitamins that put it to work
○ do many other things that scientists don't fully understand yet

There are also a few things that vitamins can't do — even though a lot of people may tell you that they can. Vitamins *can't* cure colds. Having enough vitamins in your diet can help prevent colds and other illnesses, but they won't make them go away once you catch one. The time to start drinking orange juice is before you get a cold, not after.

Also, vitamins can't give you energy. Taking lots of vitamins will not help you run faster, swim farther, or stay up later. Having enough vitamins in your diet will help you use the energy you get from other foods, but extra vitamins won't do a

thing to increase your strength or improve your
athletic performance.

From Your Plate, Not
from a Pill

Although you can buy them in bottles and jars, the
best source of vitamins is food. Since different
foods have different vitamins, the best way to
make sure you're covered is to eat a variety of
things.

So here's another time when the four food
groups come in handy. Each group has different
vitamins to offer, and by using the groups as a
guide to choosing foods during the day, you can
tell whether you're getting all of the vitamins you
need. Leave out or skimp on one of the groups,
and you'll know that your body is missing out on
some important vitamins — maybe the ones that
help keep your skin clear, your eyes bright, or
your lips from cracking and bleeding. Don't go
without one group long enough to discover what
the missing vitamins are supposed to do for you.

One tricky thing about vitamins is that they're
fragile, and foods can lose them easily. If you
cook broccoli until it's wilted and soggy, you'll destroy practically all of the vitamins. Orange juice
that's been sitting around for a few weeks and potatoes that have been skinned, steamed, then
mashed and reheated are hopeless vitamin
sources, too. In other words, the fresher the food,
and the more simply it's prepared, the more vita-

mins you'll get from it: an orange straight from its skin, for example, or raw carrots or broccoli. You get the idea.

Another way to make sure that you're getting plenty of vitamins from your food is to choose brown grain products (rice, bread, cereals) instead of white. When white flour and rice are made, most of the natural vitamins are removed from the grain. Many bread, cereal, and rice companies replace some of those vitamins by "enriching" their products. When a package says "enriched," it means that vitamins have been added to whatever's inside. But often, the vitamins that are added don't make up for the ones that have been taken out. You're better off eating foods that haven't had the vitamins removed in the first place.

Minerals

Like vitamins, minerals perform vital functions but don't carry energy. While vitamins originate in living things, minerals do not. They include water and a variety of metals and stones. You need most minerals in such small amounts that it's not worth discussing them in detail.

But four minerals deserve your attention, three because your good health and good looks depend on getting them in adequate amounts: calcium, iron, and water. The fourth, sodium, is about the only mineral that it's easy to overdo, and you'll learn why you should try to avoid getting more of it than you need.

What's in Vitamins for You

Vitamin	Needed for	Found in
A	making your bones solid and your teeth strong; seeing in the dark	carrots, sweet potatoes, cantaloupe, broccoli, spinach, apricots, nectarines, peaches, tomatoes, milk
B_1 (thiamine)	helping your system use the energy from foods; brain and nerve function	enriched cereals and breads whenever the label says "enriched with thiamine or vitamin B_1," dried beans, wheat germ, liver, oysters
B_2 (riboflavin)	helping your system use energy from foods; keeping your skin smooth; helping your eyes adjust to light	milk, yogurt, liver, broccoli, enriched cereals and breads, dried beans
B_3 (niacin)	helping your body use energy from food	chicken, turkey, tuna, eggs, enriched cereals and breads, oatmeal, brown rice, peanuts, peanut butter
B_6	helping your body use protein and fats from food; making red blood cells — needed to carry oxygen throughout your system	whole grain cereals and breads, spinach, bananas, dried beans, potatoes
B_{12}	making red blood cells	eggs, milk, yogurt, cheese, meats and fish of all kinds.
C	healing infections; keeping skin smooth; strengthening bones and teeth; helping your body use iron from foods; maybe preventing some types of cancer	citrus fruits, tomatoes, strawberries, cantaloupe, broccoli, Brussels sprouts, potatoes
D	helping your body use calcium from food	milk, yogurt, cheese, eggs
E	helping your body use and store other vitamins from foods	vegetable oils, wheat germ, whole grain cereals and breads, dried beans, spinach, broccoli, Brussels sprouts, sweet potatoes

Calcium

If you look at a number of elderly women you'll see why it's so vital to get plenty of calcium into your system. You may notice that more than a few of them are humpbacked or bent over. It's very likely that they got that way because they haven't eaten enough calcium over the years.

The hump develops when the vertebrae, tiny bones along the spine, snap. Once those bones break, there's no way to repair them, and the women who have this happen to them will never be able to stand straight again. The vertebrae aren't the only bones that break when there's a lack of calcium. All bones become fragile, and crack very easily.

Doctors are even reporting that girls who've put themselves on strict diets have been turning up with badly bent backs. The reason: not enough calcium.

Calcium:

- builds and strengthens your bones and teeth
- helps your heart keep its beat
- makes sure your blood clots so that cuts don't keep bleeding

There's simply no way your body can stand straight and strong without loads of calcium to hold the bones together. Eat enough calcium now, and you won't have to worry about ending up all stooped and misshapen.

The dairy group is the place to look for calcium.

Can You Make Your Calcium Add Up?
(You need at least 1,000 milligrams each day.)

Look back at your three-day eating chart, and check for the following foods. Add up the calcium from each of them and see if you come out with 1,000 milligrams. Don't be surprised if you don't. Many people have trouble taking in all the calcium they need.

Check for:

> milk: 300 mg for 1 cup
> yogurt: 300 mg for 1 cup
> ice milk: 150 mg for 1 cup
> broccoli: 200 mg for 1 large stalk
> sardines: 370 mg for 6 ounces
> canned salmon: 370 mg for 6 ounces
> tofu: 300 mg for 7 ounces.

(*Hint:* You can get your whole day's supply from 4 cups of milk or yogurt.)

If you're not getting enough calcium, look for ways to add it to your diet. Substitute milk for soda. Slide a slice of cheese onto your chicken, turkey, ham, or tuna sandwich. Eat yogurt instead of cookies at snacktime. Have cereal for breakfast and douse it with milk. Whenever you have fruit, cut it up and mix it with plain yogurt.

Other ways to eat more calcium:

* Melt your favorite cheese over broccoli.
* Make a double calcium shake by running milk and ice milk through the blender.
* Toss chunks of cheese into your salad. Use plain yogurt flavored with your favorite spices instead of regular dressing.
* Fix yourself hot cereal, cooking it with milk instead of water.
* Have scrambled tofu for breakfast. Scramble it just as you would an egg.

Milk, yogurt, and cheese (except cottage cheese) are among the best calcium sources. The dieters just mentioned avoided this group because they thought that dairy products are fattening. Skim dairy products — nonfat milk and yogurt, and lowfat cheeses — contain no fat or very little fat. They do contain the calcium these girls should have had to keep from ending up the way they did.

If you're allergic to milk and other dairy products, you can get your calcium from beans — kidney beans and garbanzo beans are especially high in calcium. Include them in your diet every day. Adding them to salads is one way.

Tofu, a soft, puddinglike food made from soybeans, is another good source. Like skim dairy products, tofu is low in fat and rich in protein as well as calcium.

Iron

Your body runs on energy and oxygen. Both travel through your blood, nourishing every part of your system. The way you look and feel depends a lot on how effectively your blood delivers that energy and oxygen.

What does iron have to do with this? Iron helps your blood carry oxygen through your body. When you're running low on iron, the oxygen supply slacks off, and you lose energy, concentration, and skin color. No one can expect to look, feel, or perform anything near her best if she's skimping on iron.

Iron:

o forms part of your blood that carries oxygen
  through your body
o helps release energy from food so you can
  use it

Unless you happen to love liver — one of the
few foods that carries iron in the amount you
need — you might have trouble getting enough
iron into your system. Spinach isn't the wonderful
source of iron you might think. Like most other
green vegetable sources, spinach carries other
substances that keep the iron from seeping into
your bloodstream and being used by your body.

The iron from liver, grains, eggs, meat, and
beans (like kidney and garbanzo beans) is ab-
sorbed much more easily, so those foods are better sources.

You can help your body absorb more iron by
eating a source of vitamin C along with an iron-
rich food. Vitamin C seems to break down the
chemical barriers that keep iron from making its
way into your blood. Make a spinach salad with
orange slices, and you'll get more iron from the
spinach. Have a glass of orange juice or a grape-
fruit half with a bowl of iron-enriched breakfast
cereal (Total, Bran Flakes, or Cream of Wheat are
good choices), and you'll get practically your full
day's iron requirement at breakfast. Eat a baked
potato, skin included (for vitamin C), when you're
having meat for dinner, and you'll get more iron
then, too.

Can You Make Your Iron Add Up?
(You need 18 milligrams each day.)

Look back over your three-day eating chart and check for the following foods. Add up the iron from each of them, and see if you come out with the 18 milligrams you need. Check for:

liver: 15 mg
garbanzo beans (1 cup): 7 mg
black beans (1 cup): 7 mg
Total, Kellogg's 40 Percent Bran Flakes, Cream of Wheat: 18 mg (*hint:* one bowl of any of these cereals in the morning, and you've got your iron for the day)
egg (1 large): 1 mg
kidney or pinto beans: 4 mg
spinach (1 cup): 4 mg (*hint:* use spinach in your salad instead of plain lettuce, top with garbanzo or kidney beans, and you've added about 10 mg to your iron intake)
tomato sauce cooked in an iron pot (½ cup): 80 mg
enriched rice, bread, pasta (1 cup or slice): 6 mg or so — check package to be sure

Have you figured out how to up your iron intake? What about switching to iron-enriched cereal for breakfast instead of eggs? Ask whoever does the cooking in the family to buy an iron pot and make spaghetti sauce in it once a week. Choose an iron-enriched bread for your sandwiches.

Write your iron-rich substitutions onto your chart and use them as guides as you decide what to eat each day.

Another way to guarantee you'll get enough iron is to eat foods that have been cooked in cast-iron pots. The food absorbs the iron (but not the taste of it), and passes it on to you. One cup of tomato sauce simmered in an iron pot for three hours contains enough iron for a week!

Sodium

Even though you'd die without some sodium (salt) in your system, you can get yourself into big trouble by eating too much of it. A small amount of sodium helps you hold onto the water you need for good health. But excess sodium interferes with your blood circulation and can lead to heart attacks and other problems.

Many people are used to eating foods prepared with lots of salt, and have a hard time adjusting to meals and snacks prepared without it. Adding a squirt of lemon juice or a dash of your favorite spices can make up for the flavor that you may miss when you stop putting salt on your food. Try sprinkling chili powder or pizza spice (oregano) on your popcorn instead of salt. Experiment with spices until you find those that you like the most.

You can get too much salt without going near a salt shaker. Many foods that don't seem salty contain lots of it. Most brands of corn flakes, for example, contain far more salt than you need in a day.

You need no more than 1,000 milligrams of sodium daily. A glimpse at the sodium content listed on the nutrition information label of most food packages will show you how easy it is to take in far more than that. Switch to products with little or no added salt, and encourage whoever does the shopping for the family to do the same.

Water

You could live for weeks, maybe even a month, without food (not a recommendation!), but you wouldn't last for three days without water. Water has so many jobs to do in your body, it's practically impossible to get too much of it.
Water:

- helps you use the energy you get from food
- keeps your muscles and joints flexible
- cools you off
- cleanses your system; keeps wastes from building up and making you sick
- keeps your tissues from sticking together
- fights oils and dirt that cause bad skin

You can't substitute any other type of fluid for water. Juices, special thirst-quenching potions (like Gatorade), and sodas actually work against you when you drink them instead of the water you need, draining right out of your system and taking extra, needed water with them.

Most people drink water only when they're thirsty. You may even have a hard time swallowing it when you're not. But by the time you feel thirsty, your body has already lost more water than is good for it: thirst is an emergency signal.

Put It All Together

It may seem impossible to fit all of the nutrients you need into your diet. But here are ways to put together simple meals combining them in nourishing, delicious ways.

Protein	Adding Vitamins and Minerals	Adding Fiber	Extras for Flavor
turkey or chicken (white meat, no skin)	Swiss or cheddar cheese for calcium; tomato slice for vitamins C and A	whole wheat or rye bread; baked potato with skin; lettuce	mustard (no nutrients — check the label to make sure there are no added sweeteners); mayonnaise (almost pure fat, so go easy)
peanut butter	sliced banana for vitamin A, potassium, and niacin; apple slices for vitamin A; whole wheat bread to make a "complete" protein	whole wheat bread; whole wheat crackers; apple slices	jelly, jam, honey (each adds sugar)
tuna	top with tomato and melted cheese for vitamins A and C, and calcium	whole wheat or rye bread; chopped celery	mayonnaise (nothing but fat)
eggs	scramble with cheese for calcium; make a spinach omelet for iron	sprinkle with wheat germ or bran; serve with bran muffin or whole wheat toast	
beans	cook in tomato sauce for vitamins A and C; top with cheese for calcium; serve over corn tortillas or enriched rice for a "complete" protein	beans are already loaded with fiber	salsa or taco sauce (no nutrients)

The time to drink is *before* your body has run dry — in other words, before you feel thirsty.

Doctors and nutritionists say that you should drink at least 8 cups of water a day — more when you've been working up a sweat. Water doesn't have to be dull. Try plain sparkling water; the fizzle makes it fun to drink. You can add a squirt of lemon or lime juice without interfering with the water's effect on you.

When you're playing a sport, dancing, or sunning yourself, make sure that plenty of fresh, plain water is right there with you. Whenever you pass a water fountain, pause for a sip. Have water with all of your meals, and a glass before you go to bed. You'll be surprised how quickly you get hooked.

Meals Minus Meat: Being a Vegetarian

Every vegetarian you ask will probably give you a different reason for why she or he decided to stop eating meat. Some will say that they don't think it's right for people to kill animals for food. Some will say that they're afraid of being poisoned by the chemicals that were fed to the animals to protect them from diseases and fatten them for slaughter. Still others will say that it's the easiest way to avoid cholesterol and saturated fat.

If you share any of those reasons, or have other

reasons of your own, you should know that being a healthy vegetarian involves a lot more than giving up meat. While it's certainly possible to get all of the nourishment you need without beef, pork, chicken, or fish, you can't live on lettuce and tomatoes.

Here's a rundown of the nutrients it's easy to miss in a meatless diet, along with ways you can include them:

Protein.   Because most vegetables don't contain a lot of protein, vegetarians rely on eggs, dairy products, and legumes (beans like kidney beans, garbanzos, pintos, lentils, soybeans, limas, and black-eyed peas) for the protein they need. But legumes and dairy products alone aren't adequate. They become complete protein sources only when you eat them along with something from the grain group, like rice, wheat bread, pasta, corn, tortillas, rye bread, or oats.

Calcium.   It's practically impossible to get enough calcium from vegetables alone. If you keep dairy products in your diet, you won't have to worry about finding a new calcium source. But if, like some vegetarians, you give up *all* animal products, including dairy products, you need to find other calcium sources. Start by eating tofu, a creamy, puddinglike food made from soybeans. One of the amazing things about tofu, besides the fact that it's loaded with protein and calcium, is that it has no flavor. That means that you can give it any taste you want by adding other foods and season-

ings to it. Run it through a blender with fresh fruit
and you'll have a high-calcium, high-protein, lowfat fruitshake. "Scramble" it like an egg, with
some "no stick" spray or a tiny bit of vegetable
oil, and you'll have a nourishing, calcium-rich
breakfast. Vegetarian cookbooks, including those
listed at the end of this section, recommend many
other ways to enjoy tofu.

Iron.   Since beef liver and red meat are among
the best iron sources, vegetarians who don't manage to find alternatives can get into trouble. In
fact, it's common for vegetarians to suffer from
the weakness and fatigue that come from iron deficiency.

You can spare yourself those symptoms by eating legumes like kidney beans and garbanzo beans
as often as possible, preparing tomato sauce and
other foods in cast iron pots, and including iron-
enriched grain products like bread and breakfast
cereals in your diet.

Vitamin B_{12}.   Vitamin B_{12} is just about the only
nutrient you can't get from vegetables and grains.
The consequences of going without it make a con-
vincing case for trying to get it: numbness in your
hands and feet, followed by depression and trouble concentrating, followed by — in extreme
cases — hallucinations and then total insanity.

If you eat enough dairy products, you'll be safe.
Otherwise, sprinkle B_{12} fortified brewer's yeast
onto your cereal or into your orange juice. You

can find brewer's yeast at all health-food stores and most supermarkets. Or take a vitamin pill containing 100 percent of your daily B_{12} requirement. (The label on the jar should tell you what percentage each pill contains.)

___ "But My Parents Would Freak!" ___

How well your plan to become a vegetarian goes over at home has a lot to do with how you present it and carry it out.

Most Likely to Succeed	Not Likely to Succeed
"I've just read a few articles about the way they slaughter animals for food, and I think it's really cruel and unfair. I don't like eating meat now that I know how much the animals have to suffer."	"I've just joined a cult that believes we're all reincarnated as animals, so we may be eating old Uncle Joe."
"I've been reading about the chemicals they feed to animals to make them fat. A lot of scientists don't think it's safe for us to eat animals that have been fed that stuff."	Act as though this is only a tactic to avoid your mother's cooking. Say you're a vegetarian on the nights she serves her infamous "gray goulash," then order a double cheeseburger when your family drives out to eat.
"If people didn't eat meat, there'd be a lot more food in the world to feed starving children. Right now, we waste grain by feeding it to animals, then killing the animals for food. Instead we should eat the grain ourselves and give the rest to the hungry."	Pass up dinner, eat two desserts, and call that being a vegetarian.

The way to really impress your parents (and anyone else) with the idea that you know how to eat a balanced meal without meat is to take responsible action. For one thing, you can help out with the shopping instead of putting the burden of choosing your vegetarian items on someone else.

Meatless Meals

To get you started, here are some ideas for meatless meals. Each of the food combinations on the left provides protein that's every bit as good as the protein you'd get from meat. (Remember that you have to eat both foods in order to get the protein.) The dishes listed on the right are examples of meals made from these combinations.

Combinations	Sample Meals
beans or nuts with wheat	baked beans with bread; peanut butter sandwich
lentils with rice	lentil soup with rice
beans with corn	tortillas and frijoles; tamale pie with beans
beans and rice	chili with beans over rice
whole grain cereal with milk	whole grain breakfast cereal with skim milk
pasta with cheese	macaroni and cheese; spaghetti with tomato sauce and cheese
bread and cheese	toasted cheese sandwich; pizza; cheese fondue
rice with milk	fresh rice pudding
bread with eggs	eggs and toast; french toast
peanuts with milk	peanut butter sandwich with milk

Meatless Menus		
Breakfast	Lunch	Dinner
cereal with milk or fortified soy milk, orange or grapefruit juice; whole wheat toast with peanut, cashew, or almond butter	lentil soup; whole wheat roll; carrot sticks; fresh fruit; milk or soy milk	spinach or broccoli quiche, or baked beans with brown rice; salad or mixed greens, tomatoes, and garbanzo beans
scrambled eggs or scrambled tofu; whole wheat toast; milk or soy milk; orange or grapefruit juice	leftover quiche or a sandwich made with peanut or almond butter on whole wheat bread; milk or yogurt	refried beans in corn tortillas with shredded cheese; rice; salad
whole wheat waffles with real fruit jam; milk or soy milk; orange or grapefruit juice	vegetable soup with macaroni; whole wheat roll; fresh fruit; milk or soy milk	

Make sure your shopping list includes the following:

> legumes, dried beans (black, kidney, pinto, garbanzo, soy, navy, lima, and lentils)
> whole wheat breads and crackers
> iron-enriched whole grain cereal (40 percent Bran Flakes, Total, Cream of Wheat)
> brown rice
> milk, cheese, and yogurt (if you plan to include dairy products)
> fortified soy milk* (if you won't be eating dairy products)

* Warning: Soy milk takes some getting used to.

leafy green vegetables
yellow vegetables
fresh fruit and real fruit juice

You might also plan to do your own cooking. Get yourself a few vegeterian cookbooks and experiment until you find some favorite recipes. Offer to cook for the rest of the family, and they may find that they, too, can live without meat.

Vegetarian Cookbooks

Planning vegetarian meals involves knowing, not just what foods to combine, but how much of each food to include. The books below feature delicious recipes, and give you guidelines for healthy, satisfying serving sizes.

Going Vegetarian: A Guide for Teenagers, by Sada Fretz
The Vegetarian Epicure and *The Vegetarian Epicure, Book Two,* by Anna Thomas
The Moosewood Cookbook, by Mollie Katzen
The Enchanted Broccoli Forest, by Mollie Katzen
Laurel's Kitchen, by Laurel Robertson
Diet for a Small Planet, by Frances Moore Lappé

Hurdles to a Good Diet and How to Get over Them

Now that you know what benefits come with eating fresh, nourishing foods from all four groups, it's time to tackle how to get yourself to eat what's good for you.

Here are a few of the obstacles that may spoil your plans to improve your diet:

1. Habits
2. Friends
3. Family
4. Misleading advertisements
5. Moods
6. Fast-food restaurants

You don't have to let these hurdles trip you up. Taking the following suggestions may help you get over each one.

Hurdle #1
Habits

When you don't think about what you're eating or why you're eating — you're just eating because you're used to doing it — you're eating out of habit.

You can discover your eating habits by keeping track of everything you eat for several days. Write down what you ate, when, and why you ate it. Whenever you can't come up with a "why," like "it was mealtime" or "I was hungry," it's likely that you ate out of habit.

Once you know what your habits are, you can:

1. Get rid of the habit. Let's say you're used to eating pretzels while you do your homework. Move your operation to the library or somewhere hostile to pretzel crunching. Or study with a friend who has sworn to keep you off of them.

2. Replace the eating habit with another kind of habit. If television seems bland without a bag of potato chips or nachos, do your nails or get your hands going on some knitting or sketching instead.

3. Exchange a bad food habit for a better one. If you usually eat cookies when you come home from school, switch to fruit. Have carrots instead of corn chips (they don't taste the same, but at least they crunch). Instead of buying salted, buttered popcorn, pop your own and eat it plain or sprinkled with your favorite spices.

4. Change one part of the habit: you'll probably end up changing the whole habit. For example, if you're in the habit of eating too much at mealtime, try sitting at another place at the table. The new view may give you a new attitude about how much you pile onto your plate.

Hurdle #2
Friends

Eating is contagious, and it's tough to sit there with your hands folded while your friends have theirs wrapped around tacos or fries. When you're eating out with your friends:

1. Get one of them to split an order with you. You'll save money and you'll eat only half as much junk.

2. Don't bring much money along. Unless your friends are unusually generous, they won't beg you to borrow money for a double burger and fries. Don't encourage them.

3. Get your friends to try a new place where you can get healthy foods like salads and fresh fruit. Since it can be hard to get a whole group to change its routine at once, find a place on your own, then take your friends there one by one. Once they've gotten to know it, they'll probably like the idea of going as a group.

4. Don't let your friends' habits fool you. The skinniest kid you know might also be the one who eats like a hog, making you think that you can get away with gorging yourself, too. There might be several reasons she can eat like that — maybe she's growing really fast, exercising a lot, or starving herself at home. The same goes for fat kids. It's possible for someone to eat a lot less than you, and still weigh a lot more.

Hurdle #3
Parents

While it's unlikely that your parents want you to suffer from malnourishment, you can't always count on them to make sure you're eating as well as you should.

Warning: Before you set out to make over your family's eating habits, remember that food can be a very touchy subject. Your parents may think it's enough to keep the refrigerator stocked, without having to worry about the fat, sugar, and other goop that might be in the food they supply. Also, your mother may pride herself on the way she prepares egg noodles in cream sauce from her great-grandmother's recipe, without realizing that the dish has more fat and calories than people should have today.

When it comes to trying to improve the way your family eats, take the role of educator, not dictator. And always offer to help shop, cook, and clean up.

If you want to see some changes around your house:

1. Don't tell your mother she's trying to poison you, make you fat, or give you high blood pressure. Be helpful, and pass on what you've gotten to know about the advantages of good nutrition. Volunteer to go along with whoever does the shopping in your house — here's your chance to choose skim dairy products instead of full-fat ones, fresh vegetables instead of those that come

canned or frozen in cream or butter sauce, and chicken or fish instead of fatty meats.

2. Take up cooking. Prepare your own meals instead of letting your parents get off with leaving you frozen dinners or hot dogs. If your mother does the cooking, offer to relieve her several times a week. Choose recipes that call for healthy ingredients. Once they're in the house, those ingredients may find their way into most of the meals she makes, too. (See the bibliography for cookbooks that have recipes that are not only healthy but delicious.)

3. Sabotage the cookie jar and candy bowls so you won't sabotage yourself later. Fill them with fresh or dried fruits.

4. Don't let your parents use food as a bribe. Next time, bargain for anything *but* food — a movie, magazine, album, or new clothes.

5. If your parents are overweight, don't listen to their excuses. They might blame it on a "thyroid condition" or "slow metabolism" or "genes." But in most cases, they've never gotten their eating under control or learned to enjoy regular, rigorous exercise.

You might be able to help them face up to their problem by pointing out that overweight adults are particularly prone to diabetes, heart attack, and stroke. Try to get them to go to Weight Watchers or Diet Workshop, and help them stick with their diet by keeping junk food out of the house.

But all of the encouragement in the world won't help an adult who just isn't motivated to lose weight. Don't blame yourself if your efforts fail.

And don't think that their failure means that you're destined to be fat. If you develop your own good habits, you'll become the healthy adult that they haven't managed to be.

6. On the other hand, it's no picnic to live with parents who are dieting all of the time, especially if they don't realize that you may need up to twice as many calories as they do, simply because you're growing. If you think they're being unreasonably stingy with food, suggest that your family see a registered dietitian. The dietitian will be able to tell you what each member of your family ought to be eating.

Hurdle #4
Misleading Advertising

The first thing to remember when you see ads is that the people who make them are paid lots of money to do anything and say anything to get you to buy what they're trying to sell. There are laws that are supposed to limit how far they can stretch the truth. But advertisers don't have to lie in order to give you the wrong impression. Pay attention to what ads are *really* saying. If an ad says that a drink has the "*flavor* of fresh fruit," it probably doesn't contain much (if any) *real* fruit juice. The same goes for food that are called "cheesy," or "chocolaty." Often, if you read the label, you'll find that artificial substitutes fill in for real cheese or chocolate.

Before a company puts out a new product, it hires an advertising agency to come up with an "image" for it. The image is supposed to make you think that you need that product to help your own image. The advertisers know that you'll buy the product if you think it'll make you seem more sexy, athletic, popular, smart, tough, friendly, or whatever. Depending on what image they're trying to promote, they'll come up with funny ads, "sexy" ads, ads starring famous athletes or other celebrities.

Remember, no product has an image until an advertiser gives it one. In other words, if drinking a particular brand of diet soda makes you feel like hot stuff, you're not getting that feeling from the soda, but from the way it's being advertised. Would you enjoy drinking the soda as much if a lot of fat people appeared in the ads instead of slender models?

Products that advertise the most aren't necessarily the best. Commercials are expensive, so brands that advertise a lot are simply the ones with more money to spend. Those products are usually more expensive than brands that don't advertise as much — you end up paying more so the company can afford to buy more ads.

Hurdle #5
Moods

If you eat because you're bored, lonely, or under pressure, you have to get rid of the boredom, loneliness, or stress before you can take care of the eating problems they cause.

1. Don't let yourself be bored. Take up a sport that'll keep you out of the house and away from food. Or look for part-time work that'll keep you too busy to think about snacks. Volunteer as a playground supervisor at a day-care center, or see if a local hospital needs someone to deliver flowers to patients. Rent a musical instrument and start taking lessons. Jump into an activity at school. Just don't give yourself a chance to eat your time away.

2. Don't let yourself be lonely. Loneliness comes from not sharing anything with others. Once you get involved in a sport, volunteer job, or any kind of group activity, you'll have plenty of companions with similar interests and concerns.

3. See the chapter on stress that begins on page 133.

Hurdle #6
Fast-Food Restaurants

Sometimes it seems a lot easier and a lot more fun to drop by a fast-food place for a meal than to eat at home. But most fast-food meals have more salt, more fat, and more calories than you need at one meal . . . sometimes much more than you need in an entire day. Yet few of them come close to providing the vitamins, calcium, and iron you need.

If you can't avoid eating a lot of your meals at

What's Wrong with These Meals?
Common Flaws in Fast-Food Combinations

hamburger
french fries
cola

This meal has no calcium and is very low in vitamins. You might order a cheeseburger to add calcium, or substitute milk for the cola. Make sure to drink orange juice sometime during the day, and to eat a serving of green vegetables at another meal.

fish sandwich
milkshake

This meal provides very few vitamins. Have a salad later (or earlier) in the day, and pack along some fresh fruit for dessert.

double burger (or extra-large burger) with cheese
milkshake
french fries
pie

This meal contains far too many calories and much too much fat. Have a regular cheeseburger and skip the pie. Split the fries with someone else, and share the shake by combining it with a small carton of milk and dividing it into two portions (one for a friend). You'll double the calcium in your serving and cut the calories and fat.

fast-food places, make sure to drink several glasses of milk every day, and take a multivitamin tablet with a glass of juice each morning. Order single burgers or cheeseburgers instead of the doubles or super-sizes. Do the same with tacos and burritos. Larger servings usually contain more fat, salt, and calories — not more nutrients — than smaller ones. When you order fried chicken, steer clear of "extra crispy" and peel away the skin before you eat it.

Some of the sandwiches you can order at fast-food chains are fine, if you order with the dressings on the side, and add just a dab.

Warning Signs

Watch out for "extra crispy" chicken. This almost always means that extra fat was used to prepare it.

Watch out for "special sauce." The "special" ingredients are almost always oils and sweeteners.

Watch out for "super supreme" or "deluxe" pizzas. They almost always contain globs of fatty meats and an overload of cheese.

In fact, watch out for anything that's described as being "extra special." All that usually means is that extra fat went into making it — whether it's a "King-Size Burrito," a "Whopper" burger, or a "Big Mac." Stick with "regular" or "small" orders, and you won't have to worry that fast foods will speed you along toward obesity or poor nourishment.

You don't always do yourself a favor by eating
from the salad bar or ordering a salad at fast-food
places. A ladleful of dressing can have more fat
and calories than a chocolate milkshake. Instead
of drowning it in dressing, sprinkle your salad with
cheese, add a drizzle of dressing, and stir it up
well. Add garbanzo beans (also known as chick
peas) or kidney beans for iron and protein.

Target Eating

Breakfast

Good nutrition keeps your mind sharp.

Like the rest of you, your brain must be fed in
order to work — starting with breakfast.

It's been proven time and again that students
who eat a decent breakfast do much better in
school than those who don't.

Why?

By the time you wake up, you've been going for
about ten hours without food. When lunchtime
rolls around, it may be more like fifteen hours. By
then your body is fighting for every bit of energy it
can get — just to keep itself running. It doesn't
have much to spare for your brain. You get restless, and you don't feel energetic enough to listen
to what's going on or to put any effort into your
work. If that sounds like you, maybe your attitude
toward school has a lot to do with the fact that
you're hungry for half of the day.

Eating a doughnut or some sugary cereal is almost as bad as eating nothing at all in the morning; your body uses up the sugar so that you're hungry again way before lunchtime. Bacon and sausage aren't the best choices, either. They're full of fat, which can't supply the kind of energy you need to make it until lunch. The kind of breakfast that will pull you through the morning is one that's a well-balanced meal, including foods from each of the four groups.

A lot of people who say they hate breakfast simply aren't using their imagination to plan their morning meal. If you don't happen to like cereal, eggs, milk, and juice, why not have a slice of cheese pizza? It contains many of the same nutrients and supplies the kind of energy you need to stay active and alert until lunchtime. What about a peanut butter sandwich on whole wheat with milk? Tortillas and beans with cheese? Rice pudding with raisins? A shake made by whirling milk, a banana, and a drop of vanilla extract in a blender?

If you haven't been eating breakfast, try it as an experiment for two weeks or so. You'll probably discover that school-day mornings are a lot easier to take than they were on an empty stomach.

Eating during Your Period

Your period can bring changes in your appetite as well as changes in the way your body looks and feels. The increase in hormones just before your period may make you crave sweets, salty foods, or just food in general. Many women let their eating go out of control around their periods, and end up feeling bloated and disgusted with themselves. Exercise and good nourishment help keep hormones from going haywire and giving you the kinds of cravings that make you feel gross.

If eating problems develop anyway, handle them without giving into them. If you get jittery, weak, and hungry for sweet foods, remember that the things you're going to want to eat are the things you shouldn't touch. Instead of sweets, eat crisp fresh fruits, plain popcorn, peanut butter on whole wheat toast or crackers, raisins, or yogurt. You'll feel much better.

Salt is always trouble and it can be particularly nasty right before your period. As each period approaches, you have an increase in the hormone estrogen, which has a way of making your body hold onto salt. The more salt in your system, the more water your body stores, and the more bloated you get.

If you swell up a few days before you menstruate, hold the salt. Drink lots of plain water to flush your system clean, and don't take "water pills." Those pills get rid of the fluid you need along with the extra, leaving you weak and dangerously dehydrated. Avoiding salt and drinking lots of plain water is the best way to keep water from building up and making you look and feel bloated.

Nourishing Your Skin

Acne is one of those great (well, not so great) mysteries of life. Everyone used to blame chocolate, fried foods, and cola for it. They'd say that avoiding acne was as easy as staying away from those foods.

But it turns out that acne comes from your ancestors, not from chocolate or any other food. Your zits have been passed onto you, just like your eye color and other characteristics. The most you can do for your skin is to keep it clean, drink lots of plain water, eat those fresh fruits and vegetables, and keep your hands off. You can try some of the soaps, pads, and ointments that promise to clear up your complexion, but chances are they won't work.

A better plan would be to save your money for a visit to a dermatologist, who can give you a safe treatment that does work.

Weight-Loss Diets

Putting yourself on a diet while you're growing can be like letting a seedling go without water. You can't develop normally without the proper nutrients, and you can't get those nutrients without eating daily portions of a variety of foods.

The only time you should consider a weight-loss diet is when your doctor tells you to. And then you should follow the diet your doctor recommends, not one you find in a magazine or hear about from friends.

Why You Might Feel Fat Even When You're Not

It's easy to mistake the extra padding you develop during puberty for genuine fat. When you're used to having a perfectly straight little-girl's body, the sight of this soft, new flesh around your hips, stomach, and breasts may be enough to scare you into a starvation diet. But chances are you aren't really getting fat, and that the extra padding will vanish as you mature.

What If the Fat Is for Real?

Even if you are getting too heavy (and only your doctor can tell you this for sure) starving yourself is not the way to get your weight under control. In fact, most doctors think that over-weight teenagers shouldn't try to lose weight at all, but should, instead, hold their weight steady until they've grown into it. They do this by eating foods from all four groups, keeping portions small, and avoiding all fats and most sweets. But they don't set out to see the numbers on the scale drop. Trying to lose weight while you're growing is just too dangerous, even for girls who should be many pounds less than they are.

Five Good Reasons Not *to Put Yourself on a Diet*

Reason #1.   You'll feel lousy because you won't have enough energy to do the things you enjoy. Also, you'll feel as if you're punishing yourself.

Reason #2.   You may damage your body and end up worse off than you think you are now. Remember the reasons you need calories:

- to grow
- to keep your body processes going (heart, lungs, digestion, brain)
- to let you be active and alert

When you don't eat, there simply aren't enough calories to go around.

Reason #3.   Exercise has it all over dieting as a way to get in shape. Here's why:

- Exercise firms and redistributes weight, so even if you don't lose any of it, the weight you've got will look a lot better.

○ Exercising burns calories, not just while you're at it, but afterward. If you exercise often enough to develop firm muscles, you'll burn more calories just sitting still than you would otherwise.

○ Studies have shown that the difference between fat girls and thinner ones is not what they eat. The difference is what they do: thin girls move, fat girls don't.

Reason #4. You may end up gaining weight, anyway, especially if you try to lose weight by:

○ Not eating at all. Sooner or later you'll get so hungry that you'll lose control and put away more in an hour than you'd normally eat in a week.

○ Sticking to one food. Soon you'll be so bored that you'll give up.

○ Skipping breakfast and lunch. By late afternoon you'll be pigging out.

It's more sensible, and effective, to control your weight by eating small portions of a variety of foods from each of the groups on your three-day chart.

Reason #5. You'll be a real drag around your friends because you'll be so caught up in your diet you won't talk about anything else. No one wants to hear about how fat you are.

What If You Really Do Weigh Too Much?

It's one thing to think that you're overweight and another to have your doctor say that you are. If that happens, the first thing to do is get yourself motivated to watch your weight.

- ✿ Make a list of reasons to be thin. Don't borrow anyone else's reasons; make each of them your own. Now make up a list of reasons to be fat. If you end up with more reasons in favor of fat than against it, go back to your soda and corn chips and forget the whole thing. Otherwise, post it on the cupboards, refrigerator, or wherever it will best remind you that you really want to be thin.

- ✿ Go to the supermarket and head for the flour. How much overweight are you? Ten pounds? Fifteen? Pick up a sack of flour (or two) that weighs as much as your extra flab. Carry it around the store until you're about to drop. Trudge back to the flour shelf and put the sack(s) down. Feel relieved? That's how you'll feel when your body is no longer carrying around the same amount of flab.

- ✿ Go public. Tell a few choice people that you're going to transform yourself. Make sure they're the kind of people who will make life miserable for you if you don't follow through.

- ✿ Sign a contract with a relative who wants to help (nagging is *not* helping). In the contract, you promise to control your weight exactly according to the doctor's orders. The relative agrees to buy you some clothes when you reach a new size, take you somewhere, or give in on some rule you don't like.

- ✿ Write notes to yourself. Be as nasty or as supportive as you want, then stick them around where you can't miss them.

_____Dumb Excuses for Overeating_____

"*I ate one already, so I might as well eat them all.*"

You get fat by eating too many calories. The more calories you eat, the fatter you'll get. The best thing to do when you start to overeat is to *stop*.

"*I don't want to hurt the cook's feelings, so I'd better have seconds.*"

Who's the one getting hurt here? Does Mom or Grandma or Mrs. Jones have to stand around the locker room watching as two kids demonstrate that both of them can fit into her gymsuit?

Don't let anyone make you feel guilty for trying to protect your body. It's *your* body. You have the last words — and when it comes to dessert, they should be "No, thank you."

It helps to practice some good, firm refusals. Always include a compliment, and something like "I *would* eat more if I could, but I'm too full to even think about it now." Better not mention your diet, because they'll probably say something totally untrue, like "You're just pleasantly plump. You don't need to lose weight."

Here are some more refusals:

"Thank you, but I think I've had more than enough already. Please offer the rest to somebody else."

"Your chocolate-coated corn fritters are excellent, Mrs. Balboa, but one is all I can handle, thank you."

"You're right, Grandma, I usually have two pieces of your cake. It's as good as ever, but I'm just not as hungry as usual."

"I'll diet tomorrow."

Now you're thinking of your diet as punishment, when eating properly and getting yourself in shape should be something you're glad to do for yourself. Food is fun for the few moments it's in your mouth, but a good-looking, healthy body is fun all of the time.

"It's a special occasion."

While everyone else is putting away the ice cream and cake, remember that you won't have much to celebrate if you have to spend the rest of your life under a few layers of fat. Get yourself a glass of diet soda or sparkling water. If you are *dying* for some cake, have a sliver and eat it s-l-o-w-l-y. At big family celebrations like Thanksgiving, Passover, Christmas, or Easter, have small portions of just about everything (you might skip the gravy and butter). Hold your ground when well-meaning relatives insist that you eat, eat, eat. Remember who'll end up wearing the fat home.

Dieting Can Get out of Control . . .

and lead to stunted growth, baldness, scaly skin, broken bones, and lifelong emotional problems.

No one knows why some girls become addicted to diets while others have trouble sticking to one for more than a day. But here's how a "diet addiction" might start.

For some reason "Lori" decided to go on a diet. Maybe it was because one of the guys at school teased her about her hips. Maybe it was because she wanted to look more like her skinny friend Natalie. Or maybe it was because she wanted to prove that she could do it.

Whatever her reason, once she started losing weight, she couldn't stop.

Her hips vanished with the first ten pounds. But she didn't seem to notice that they were gone. Everytime she ate something, she could swear she saw her hips bulging out again. She'd look in the mirror and see flab where her family and friends saw nothing but a skeleton.

Her best friend told her she was being a jerk, but Lori ignored her; she thought that her friend was just jealous of her willpower. Whenever her mother tried to get her to eat, she accused her mom of trying to make her fat. She'd lie and sneak — anything to keep from eating. She thought about only two things: how to avoid food and how to get exercise.

Lori thought she was making herself fit, but she was turning into a wreck. Being hungry all the time was making her irritable and impatient. Dangerous changes were occurring inside her body, too. Her heart beat was getting much too slow, her bones were getting thin and weak, and her periods, which had started just a few months before, stopped.

Lori was suffering from anorexia nervosa, which you could describe as an addiction to dieting. Again, no one knows why some girls get anorexia while others don't — but just about everyone agrees that anorectics need professional help if they are to recover.

Here's another type of eating problem.

Like Lori, "Cheryl" was scared of gaining weight. But she handled her fear very differently. Instead of starving herself, she ate her way through gallons of ice cream, entire cakes, loaves of bread, and boxes of cereal. When she'd reach the point where she couldn't cram another morsel down her throat, she'd run to the bathroom and heave it all into the toilet.

At first she did it just once in a while, for "fun." But then she started to panic about her weight, and made herself throw up after every meal. She was wasting tons of food and loads of time. And she was losing confidence in herself. She became so disgusted with herself that she stopped going out with friends. She'd call off plans because she couldn't stand to face anyone, knowing that she'd spent a good part of the day stuffing herself and vomiting.

Everyone knew she was acting weird, but no one could tell that she was suffering from bulimia, another eating problem that, like anorexia, needs attention from a doctor with experience in that area.

You May Have an Eating Problem If Two or More of These Remind You of Yourself

- ❏ You think you can actually see fat appear right after you've eaten.
- ❏ One or two parts of your body (hips, thighs) seem really gross to you, and you feel you have to keep dieting to get rid of them.
- ❏ Most of the time you're thinking about food and how to get out of eating it.
- ❏ You spend more time exercising than doing anything else outside of school, but you never feel you've exercised enough.
- ❏ Everyone's telling you that you're thin enough, but you think they just want you to be as fat and out of shape as they are.
- ❏ You spend a lot of time in the supermarket looking at food you'd rather die than eat. You read recipes for things you wouldn't touch because they're "too fattening."
- ❏ You worry that other people are deliberately putting fattening things into your food.
- ❏ You think you have to stay thin to prove yourself. The second you let up on your diet, everyone will know that you're a failure.
- ❏ If you could choose between looking like a lean teenage boy and a well-developed woman, you'd pick the boy.
- ❏ You won't go out with friends when you think they might make you eat something.
- ❏ Whenever someone offers you food, you make up an excuse to get out of eating it.
- ❏ You think you probably need help, but you're afraid that they'll make you get fat.

What to Do If You Recognize Yourself in the Examples Above

What would you do if you suspected you had pneumonia, malaria, or cancer? You'd go to a doctor.

Eating disorders are just as harmful and can be just as deadly. They need just as much attention.

Doctors who specialize in eating disorders don't want you to get fat any more than you do. They *do* want to help you feel confident enough to nourish yourself properly.

What if your parents think that you need a few milkshakes more than you need professional help? Confide in an adult you trust, and have her or him plead your case with your folks. Someone must help them understand that you can't solve your problem on your own, no matter how much they encourge you.

Treatment for eating disorders usually involves discovering that the fear of fat is hiding fears of other things. A good doctor will help you face up to those fears so you won't waste the rest of your life worrying about how much you weigh.

But Be Careful

Once you've decided to go for help, don't call up any old clinic or doctors advertising as "eating disorder specialists." Get your own doctor to refer you to one, or call the adolescent clinic at your local hospital and ask for a referral.

If the doctor you see wants to put you in the hospital for treatment, see another doctor (at a different hospital) for a second opinion before you allow yourself to be admitted. If both agree that you should be hospitalized, it might be best to move in for a while. Otherwise, you may be better off getting help on an "outpatient" basis, that is, going into the hospital for appointments but not for a stay.

3

Get Up and Go

What Exercise Will Do for You

Exercise does so many great things for you, you may not be aware of them all. Test your knowledge with this quiz — and be prepared for some surprising answers.

1. Which is a truly safe, dependable, and effective way to get yourself to eat less?

    a. Take diet pills.
    b. Swear off breakfast and lunch.
    c. Exercise every day.

Answer: "C" is correct. Exercise is the best way to keep your appetite under control. When you exercise, your brain sends out a hormone that blocks the hormones that make you hungry. If you don't move around much, the "hunger hormones" just keep coming. So when people say exercise makes you build up an appetite, they're wrong.

"A" is dangerously wrong. Diet pills can upset your system in a number of ways. Some affect your ability to smell and taste. Some keep you from sleeping. Many make you weak, irritable, and dizzy. You can get addicted to them. Besides, they're usually ineffective.

"B" is hazardous because you'd become weak and irritable as the day went on. It's also impractical, because you'd probably be so hungry by late afternoon that you'd eat more then than you would have at both meals combined.

2. In most cases, thin girls stay thin and fat girls get fatter because:

    a. The fat girls eat more.
    b. The thin girls have a higher metabolism.
    c. The thin girls exercise a lot more.

Answer: "C" is correct. Studies have shown that the only difference between fat teenage girls and thin ones is the amount of moving around they do. While you exercise, you're using up energy that would otherwise turn into fat. If you exercise a lot, your body will burn off more energy even while you're sitting still. People who don't exercise burn off very little of the food energy they take in, and it ends up as fat.

Exercise also makes you look thinner because it tones your muscles. Muscles hold your skin firm instead of letting it go flabby.

3. When you're upset, you can make yourself feel better fast by:

    a. Sleeping it off.
    b. Having a chocolate bar and a cola chaser.
    c. Going for a walk, swim, run, or bike ride.

Answer: "C" is correct. Getting up and moving around will do the most to help you lose the tension you feel when you're under pressure. Exercise stops or slows the flow of stress hormones, so there's a very real improvement in the way you feel once you start moving. Also, it will help get your mind away from what's bothering you, and give you the sense that you have some control over the way you feel.

Sleep doesn't often help. Waking up to your problems can be depressing enough to make you want to go right back to bed.

Eating usually makes things worse, too. Sweets, especially, give you a rush of good feeling, but leave you hungry and irritable not long afterward.

4. The best way to deal with menstrual cramps is:

    a. Take pills for the pain.
    b. Lie in bed.
    c. Exercise all month every month.

Answer: "C" is correct. Exercise — before, during, and after your period — helps you avoid menstrual problems. Most of those problems come from hormone imbalances that exercise can correct. Some girls use cramps as an excuse not to exercise. Actually, they are one of the best reasons *to* exercise.

Pills are okay every once in a while — when you're desperate. But it's not good for your body to become dependent on pain relievers. You may suffer side effects from the pills worse than the pain that they're supposed to get rid of. Besides, they're expensive.

Lying in bed, inactive, may only make your cramps worse.

5. Your skin tends to break out a lot. You no sooner get rid of one monster zit than two more crop up on your face. Which is the best way to keep acne under control?

> **a.** Eat lots of fresh fruits and vegetables.
> **b.** Drink plenty of water (at least 8 cups each day)
> **c.** Get lots of exercise.

Answer: All three are correct. The combination of a wholesome diet, lots of water, and daily exercise not only helps protect your skin from problems, but keeps the rest of you looking and feeling your best, too.

Getting Started

Just knowing that exercise is the simple solution to weight problems, skin trouble, depression, and

menstrual cramps may be enough to get you
going. But what if it's not? What if you still feel
you'd rather be fat, or risk a dangerous diet, than
run every day? What if you'd rather have cramps
once a month than swim laps three times a week?

Many people have two complaints about exercise.

1. It's boring.
2. It hurts.

If you feel that way, it's probably because you
haven't tried enough activities to find one you enjoy. Give yourself a chance to discover that you
get more fun from moving than from sitting
around — that your body feels much better when
you're using it than when you're not.

You're apt to get bored and uncomfortable jog-
ging in worn-out sneakers in a dull part of town in
the middle of a hot summer day. That's hardly the
way to discover the joy of fitness. You might be
more motivated by dancing on ice skates; playing
in a soccer, basketball, hockey, or lacrosse league;
or practicing water ballet, gymnastics, or tap
dancing. The idea is to have fun while you're
moving — not to torture yourself into shape.

Finding a Sport

The two most important things to consider when
you're choosing an athletic activity is how much

movement it involves, and how much fun it is for you. The only way exercise can help you is if it keeps your whole body in motion and if you like it enough to do it several times a week.

Sports sometimes come in fads, and you may want to get involved in a particular activity just because it's the one that everyone else is doing. Going for a popular sport can be a good way to get involved in athletics. But it can also be frustrating and discouraging. If you find you're not especially good at whatever it is, you may feel like giving up on athletics altogether. If something like that happens to you, look around until you find a sport that you can do and that you enjoy. Trends don't last, but the effects of a good exercise program do.

At the same time, it may take you a while to discover how good you are at something. When you find a sport that appeals to you, you can't expect to be great when you just start out. Stick with it until you get past the awkward stage to a point where you're having fun, *or* until you're absolutely positive you'll never catch on.

Where to Look

○ Go to games, meets, and matches. This is especially easy if you live near a college with a good athletic program. Watch as many different sports being played as you can. When you've seen a few that appeal to you, find out how you can get involved at your own level.

Where can you get training? Is there a league for your age group? It's likely that one of the college coaches, or your own gym teacher, could help you get this information.

o Watch sports on television, especially shows like "Wide World of Sports," which covers an incredible variety of athletic events.

o Drop in on classes. Pick up a schedule from your local YWCA or YMCA, Girls' Club, or recreation center, and sit in on dance, martial arts, water ballet, or other movement classes until you find one (or more) that you can't resist.

Any sport you choose will have its advantages and drawbacks. Here is a rundown of some of the more popular athletic activities, including their strengths and weaknesses. You'll also find some "hints" to help you get the most exercise value from each of the sports on this list.

What's Stopping You?

Some people have a block against exercise. They've heard all about how much good it can do for them, but for some reason the message never sinks in. The reason may be that they've been getting other messages that make exercise seem risky, pointless, or painful.

If you're not particularly excited about working

Pros and Cons of Popular Sports

Sport	Advantages	Drawbacks	Hints
Running	Just about the best for endurance, for getting your pulse rate up, and for putting fresh oxygen into your system. It's something you can do your whole life, and it doesn't cost much — just enough to buy a pair of spongy-soled running shoes and some thick athletic socks. Running is convenient; you can do it whenever you want, and you can do it alone.	It can be dull, especially if you live in a drab part of town. Unless you're able to use an indoor track, you can get rained out a lot. Also, running can be jarring, putting strain on bones and tendons. In fact, runners tend to develop more injuries than football players.	Warm up by stretching before you run. Run for at least fifteen minutes (not including the stretching time). If you're running outdoors, take different routes so you won't get bored. Try to talk as you run. If you have to gasp, you're going too fast. Land on your heels and spring from your toes — don't land on flat feet. If you get thirsty along the way, drink plain water or fruit juice diluted with water. Wind down after you run by walking and stretching again. Run at least three times a week. For safety, run during daylight hours.
Bicycling	Another good way to get your endurance and heart rate up if you keep pedaling and you cover a course that's at least three miles long or includes a few steep hills. It's convenient because you can do it alone, on your own time. You can also use the bike for	It can be expensive. A good bike, helmet, lock, and other accessories add up. It can be dangerous (if not impossible) during foul weather and wherever there's heavy traffic.	Warm up as you ride by starting slowly and building speed gradually. Check to be sure your bike "fits" you: Get someone to hold the bike upright so you can sit with both feet on the pedals. Push one pedal down as if you were going to ride, stopping when

Activity	Benefits	Drawbacks	Tips
	or wherever. It's something you can do throughout your life, and it's guaranteed to do good things for your legs.		perfectly straight, and your foot should be flat on the pedal. Be sure to wear a helmet whenever you're riding in traffic. Have a headlight and several reflectors for night riding. Learn the rules of the road, including hand signals to let cars know when you're turning.
Basketball, hockey, soccer, and lacrosse	Good for endurance because you're moving constantly while at play. Also terrific for coordination and skill. Since they're team sports, you get motivation from the other players.	Not particularly convenient; you can't get up a game by yourself. You probably won't be able to play any of these sports throughout your life.	To get anything out of these sports, you must play — as opposed to sitting on the sidelines — at least three times each week. Keep yourself in condition by working out with weights, running, or jumping rope.
Tennis and other racquet sports	Good for coordination and skill. Can be good for endurance if you can keep a game going steadily for fifteen minutes or more. Good for your social life — making plans to play tennis is one of the easiest dates you can arrange.	You can't count on racquet sports for an adequate workout. Unless you're really good and you're playing with someone who's just as good, you won't move steadily enough to test your endurance and raise your heart rate. It can be expensive — racquets, clothing, and court time may run over your budget.	You'll have a stronger, faster game if you also run, jump rope, or work out with weights. Make sure you know what the dress code is wherever you're going to play — there's nothing like getting kicked off the court for wearing the "wrong" shoes. Whenever possible, play with someone better than you; your game will improve as you try to keep up.

Sport	Advantages	Drawbacks	Hints
Swimming	Great for endurance when you swim for twenty minutes or more. It's the one exercise that uses almost all of your muscles, so you get a complete workout. It's soothing, and you can do it for the rest of your life.	Can be inconvenient if the nearest pool *isn't* near. Your eyes and skin may be sensitive to chlorine.	Use different strokes so you won't get bored. Ask a coach or another swimmer to show you how to use weights and paddles so you can get more out of your swim. Get a one-piece racing suit, making sure that it's not too tight anywhere. Pick up a pair of goggles and adjust them so water can't seep in. Protect your hair by coating it with conditioner and covering it with a bathing cap before you dive in. The conditioner will rinse out in the shower afterward.
Gymnastics	One of the better ways to develop strength, flexibility, and coordination. Because it is a high-pressure sport, you learn how to handle stress and develop self-confidence.	Can be inconvenient and expensive unless you have easy access to good coaching and equipment at a low fee. You need endurance for gymnastics, but you have to get it from some other kind of athletic activity like running. It's dangerous without expert su-	Look for an experienced coach. Perhaps your gym teacher can help you find one, or check under "Gymnastic Instruction" in the Yellow Pages phone directory.

...country skiing	...for endurance, coordination, and strength. Cross-country skiing works on your arms and legs, and both skating and skiing do all of the things a good workout is supposed to do.	...fall is rare and "ice time" at indoor rinks costs a fortune.	...riding and roller-skating can help keep you in condition during the "off" season.
Dancing	A good choice for endurance and coordination. Music gets you motivated and keeps you moving. It's convenient because you can do it alone. Dance lessons are inexpensive and easy to find. You can get a decent workout at a party or dance where you have a partner who can keep up with you.	Music makes noise — your family and neighbors might rather have you go running.	Dance for at least twenty minutes three times a week. Warm up by stretching to some easygoing music, then put on something more rowdy. If you want a structured routine, look under "Dance Instruction" or "Exercise Classes" in the Yellow Pages phone directory, or see what's being offered at the local YWCA or Girls' Club.
Rowing	Like swimming, it works on just about all of your muscles. Rowing with a team, you get motivation and discipline from the rest of the group. Rowing alone, you can enjoy the serenity of the water and the freedom to set your own pace.	Can't do it all year long in places where the water freezes over. Can't do it at all where there is no water. The equipment is expensive.	Row at least three times a week for twenty minutes each time. Pace yourself so you won't get pooped before it's time to head back. Make sure someone knows you're in the water, and have a life vest with you at all times.

Sport	Advantages	Drawbacks	Hints
Weight training	A sure way to make your muscles stronger and develop flexibility. You'll be able to see a difference in your shape within weeks after you start working out; you'll find that you're firm where you may have been flabby.	Doesn't increase endurance or raise heart rate. In other words, it's a good way to supplement an exercise program but it shouldn't *be* your exercise program. Can be inconvenient and expensive, depending upon how close and costly a weight-training facility is.	Work out no more than three times a week, and never work out two days in a row. Your muscles and bones need time to recover from the strain of the extra weight. Don't have weight-lifting contests with your friends or try to teach yourself how to lift; you can ruin your bones for life. Get expert instruction from a trainer or coach. Check your local Y and area health clubs for lessons and supervision.
Horseback riding	Good for endurance, strength, and coordination. Hard to think of anything more exhilarating and refreshing. Riding in shows is a high-pressure sport that helps you develop self-confidence and stress-management skills.	Probably the most expensive sport there is. It won't do anything for you unless you work at it; it's easy to let the horse do the work for you.	Ride rigorously at least three times a week. Strengthen your legs with weights. Get to know the temperament of any horse before you mount and ride.

Sports that develop skill but not fitness:
  Archery
  Bowling
  Fishing
  Golf
  Riflery

out — even though you know what a difference
it'll make in the way you look and feel — maybe
you've heard too many discouraging words about
exercise. Here are a couple of them, as well as
reasons you shouldn't let them get in your way.

❝*Running or other strenuous exercise is dangerous. You can
hurt yourself.*❞

Sure you can hurt yourself. Some athletes are
always turning up with sprains, cuts, strains, dis-
locations, and fractures. But their injuries don't
come from what they're doing — they come from
the way they do it. They jump in too fast, take on
too much, or keep at it too long.

You can stay safe by warming up before you
begin. Stretching helps prevent sprains, strains,
and fractures. If you're new to a sport, don't try
to keep up with your friends who've been at it for
years. Build up to their speed gradually. Make
sure you have the proper equipment and that it fits
as it should. Safety gear can be expensive, but a
bicycle helmet, for example, is a lot less costly
than brain surgery.

If you get hurt, see a doctor right away. *Never*
try to "work through" an injury, even if your
coach advises you to do it. Tell the coach you'd
rather wait for your doctor's instructions, and then
do exactly as the doctor says.

Marathons are not for growing bodies. The ten K
is the maximum distance you should run while
you're still developing. Marathons take too much
energy from bones and cells that need it for

growth, so you're better off waiting until you've reached your full height, when you'll have energy to spare to cover that distance.

❝Exercise has to hurt. No pain, no gain.❞

You don't have to hurt your body to help it, and anyone who says you do is leading you to trouble.

Pain during or after exercise indicates that something is wrong. Either you're overdoing it, or you've injured yourself.

All it takes to get something from exercise is effort. Making an effort means getting your body to move faster or work harder than it does under normal conditions. How much harder? Enough to feel yourself breathing harder (but not losing breath and gasping for it) and to raise your pulse. A high pulse means that your heart is getting a workout, too.

Before you start moving, check your pulse. Find your pulse by taking the index and middle fingers of your right hand and pressing them lightly over the wrist, just below your left hand. (If you're left-handed, you can use the fingers of your left hand over the wrist of your right.) Don't use your thumb, because it has a tiny pulse of its own that could confuse things.

Once you've found your pulse, register how fast it's moving. You should feel it thump about 70 times in one minute when your body is at rest. Once you've been exercising for ten minutes, pause briefly to check your pulse again. You should feel it thump at least 100 times in one minute. If not, you have to put more effort into your workout until it does.

What You Can Expect from Exercise

Right Away

You'll feel good. Exercise works on the part of your brain that determines what kind of mood you're in. No matter how rotten you feel when you start out, a good run, swim, bike ride, or walk will cheer you up. If you're already feeling good, you'll feel even better.

After a Few Weeks

Your body will be firmer and more flexible. Your pulse will be slower when you're not working out, a sign that your heart is working at a healthier pace. You'll look better; the difference will start to show in your shape, your skin, and your outlook on life.

What You Can't Expect from Exercise

You can't expect to look like the models you see in magazines and advertisements. Let's put it this way — if you went to take voice lessons, you'd expect your voice to improve, but you wouldn't go into it thinking that you'd turn out sounding exactly like the top-selling female vocalist. The same goes for your shape, which is exactly how it should be. You'll end up with *your* body in shape — not with the shape of anyone else.

A Workout That Works

The word *exercise* covers a lot of different activities, from walking to weight lifting. The best exercise is any kind that keeps your whole body moving for at least twenty minutes, makes you breathe harder than usual, and gets your heart going faster.

A good exercise routine involves these four things:

Stretching.   This softens and relaxes your muscles, preparing them to handle the extra stress you put on them during your workout. Well-stretched joints are less likely to strain, break, or sprain. Five minutes of stretching could prevent five weeks in a cast.

Warming up.   Before you begin working out at full tilt, start slowly, using the same motions you'll be using when you're really going. By starting out easy, you're giving your blood time to make its way to your muscles. The blood is fuel for those muscles, and if you don't give it a chance to get to them, they'll poop out on you.

Conditioning.   This is when you work your body so that you feel a difference in your pulse rate and in the way you're breathing. During conditioning, you're working out the most important muscle of all — your heart. Exercise that increases your pulse rate (makes your heart beat faster) is the kind that has all of the benefits mentioned before, like controlling your appetite and making you feel more cheerful.

It also has another terrific benefit: it makes your body burn energy — not just while you're working out, but afterward, too. And that helps prevent fat. People who don't get conditioning exercise end up storing much more of what they eat as fat than people who work out often. The reason for this is that muscles that are in good shape from conditioning use up a lot of energy. Fat uses hardly any energy at all. That's because muscles work, holding your skin firm and helping you move. Fat just sits there.

Here are some conditioning sports:

> basketball
> bicycling
> cross-country skiing
> dancing
> field hockey
> lacrosse
> running

skating
soccer
swimming
walking swiftly

Cooling Down.   Don't bring yourself to a dead stop when you've finished your workout. Your body isn't prepared to quit as quickly as you might be, and the result of a sudden halt could be cramps, dizziness, or even fainting. Slow to a stop by lightly doing whatever activity you've been doing. Once you've stopped, do a few stretches to complete the cooldown.

Warning: *Never* get into a hot shower until you have cooled down completely. Here's why: While you're working out, your blood circulates to the muscles you are using. During your cooldown, your blood begins to circulate more evenly through your system. Hot water makes the blood come to your skin. If you get under hot water before you've cooled down and gotten the blood flow back to normal, your blood will be confused. It will rush to your skin, suddenly leaving the rest of you without enough to work normally. You could faint as a result. The shower is not a terrific place to faint. You could easily crack your skull, or even drown.

Every Other Day

You've already read, many times, that you should find a sport or athletic activity that you enjoy. One reason for this is that you won't get any conditioning effect from a workout you do only once or even twice a week. You should find something that you enjoy enough to do at least every other day, or, in other words, three times a week.

Some people think they can save time by doing a long, hard workout once a week instead of several shorter, lighter workouts throughout the week. Actually, that kind of workout is a waste of time. One workout can't produce any of the results of a conditioning program that involves twenty minutes (or more) of constant motion at least three times a week.

Not Too Fast

Then there are other people who think that the idea of working out three times a week is to make each workout tougher than the one before. These people add distance each time they run, or tack on an extra lap each time they swim, or spend an additional minute or so on the exercise bicycle. While a routine has to be a challenge for your body, it doesn't have to, and shouldn't, get more difficult by the day.

Changes in your routine should be gradual, to allow your muscles and the rest of your system to get strong enough to handle them. Never add an entire mile onto your running distance at once. Take a few weeks to build up to it. The same goes for every other activity. Don't push yourself to go far beyond what you're doing now — take it slowly and you'll get there in much better shape.

How to Get Yourself Going

How much you get out of exercise has a lot to do with how much you enjoy doing it. Here are some suggestions that might make working out more fun for you.

○ Get a friend to go along. Work out together and keep track of each other's progress. Set up an exercise schedule, and reward yourselves for each week that you manage to stick to it.

○ Get some special exercise clothes. They don't have to be the expensive snazzy kind, just an outfit that you're comfortable wearing. Don't even think about putting it on unless you're going to be working out.

○ If your workout involves running, biking, or walking, head off toward someplace fun, like a park or a friend's house.

○ Put off doing something you want to do (phoning a friend, eating, watching television) until you've exercised.

○ Set goals for yourself. It's fun to keep track of your progress, and you'll have more progress to record if you keep each goal just slightly tougher than what you've been able to do already. Big goals can be discouraging, and — if they involved pushing yourself much harder than usual — they can be dangerous.

Choosing a Goal

There are four types of goals you can choose among.

1. Distance goals: you can challenge yourself to go farther than you've gone before.
2. Speed goals: you can see if you can move faster than before.
3. Endurance goals: you can see if you can last longer — spend more time in motion.
4. Repetition goals: you can challenge yourself to repeat an exercise more than before. For example, try for thirty sit-ups if you've been doing twenty-five.

Life in Motion:
Get Your Body Involved

The kind of exercise you get from sports and athletics is just one type of movement that's important to the way you grow, look, and feel. The other is movement you work into your day by walking instead of taking rides, climbing stairs instead of riding elevators, and generally using your body instead of relying on vehicles and appliances to transport you and take care of certain tasks. Not that you should revert to the Stone Age. There will always be times when it wouldn't make sense to try to get somewhere or do something on your own steam.

But there will also be plenty of times when you wouldn't be sacrificing anything — and, in fact, would be gaining a great deal — by getting more movement into your life. The greatest benefit is that you'd stay in good shape. Your body gets better with use, so the more you rely on it during each day, the more it improves.

What's more, you'll want to stay in shape. As you depend more and more on your body, you'll realize that it works and feels best when it's well rested and well nourished.

An Attitude Quiz

Here's a quiz to help you discover how you feel about using your body. Afterward, you'll learn how to use your answers as a guide to improvement.

1. You're about to get onto an elevator. It's positively jammed. There is a staircase that would take you to the floor you want. You:

> **a.** Wedge yourself into the elevator.
> **b.** Decide to wait for the next car.
> **c.** Charge up the stairs.

2. You're walking to school, and halfway there Mrs. Balboa drives up and offers you a ride. You:

> **a.** Take it. Why walk when you can ride?

   b. Take it because you don't want to hurt her feelings.

   c. Thank her, but say that you're enjoying your walk.

3. When playing volleyball in gym class, your strategy is to:

   a. Wait for the ball to hit you before you hit back.

   b. Wait for the ball to come, then duck.

   c. Run to meet the ball and slam it.

4. You just sat down to do your homework, and you realize that the only thing you have to write with is a fat purple magic marker. You:

   a. Turn in homework done in purple magic marker.

   b. Yell to someone to bring you a pen from the next room.

   c. Get up and go into the next room to get the pen for yourself.

5. You're baby-sitting for the Conroy kids, who aren't allowed to play outside unless you're with them. They want to play outside. You:

   a. Tell them they can stay up extra late if they'll stay inside and watch television.

   b. Send them out alone and just pray they don't wander in front of a moving truck.

   c. Go out and play with them.

6. When you go to the pool on a hot day, you:

   a. Dive in to cool off, then lie sunning yourself for the next few hours.

   b. Jump in over and over, just to splash the lifeguard and catch his attention.

   c. Swim laps or play water tag.

The answers to these questions should help you discover how much you put your body into what you do from day to day. If you came up with "c" most of the time, you're probably pretty active, and, consequently, in good, if not excellent, shape.

The "c" answers indicate that you naturally enjoy using your body, and that you rely on it to help you get things done.

The other answers suggest that you prefer to have things done for you, and that you'd do almost anything to avoid moving. If that's the way you feel, you're letting your body go to waste.

Remind Yourself to Move

If your body doesn't automatically get up and do things for you (if, for example, it just waits for someone else to bring you a pen, or for the volleyball to come your way), you have to keep after it until it does.

Remind yourself to move, and before long you won't have to think about it anymore. Think twice before you accept a ride. Get up and do things you usually ask someone else to do for you. Start taking the stairs instead of waiting for crowds to thin out of escalators or elevators. When you're watching television, don't just sit there; let the commercials remind you that it's time to get up and move around.

Where Bad Attitudes Begin

It may be easier to develop good movement attitudes once you know where bad ones come from. Think about it and you'll realize that you've heard some pretty dumb things about movement, things that can make you want to forget the whole idea. Here are some of them, along with reasons you should ignore them.

❝_What do you think cars are for? Why walk when you can ride?_**❞**

Cars, escalators, elevators — all of the gizmos that make life easier for you — can make things a lot worse for your body. Your body works best for you when you make it work. Every time you use your legs to get around you're toning up your muscles, burning off some calories, and giving your spirits a lift.

Of course you shouldn't plan to walk everywhere. Just don't become dependent on power-driven vehicles. Walk, bike, run wherever you can. Whenever you have to be somewhere, plan to set out early so you won't end up catching a ride just to make it on time. Get someone to walk or bike along with you, and find a route that's interesting and safe.

"Careful not to overdo it!" or *"You must be exhausted after taking that test. Why don't you just stay and relax instead of going off on your bike?"*

Words like that can make you feel tired before you begin. Not that it's impossible to overdo it, but you have to discover your own limits. Pay attention to what your body's telling you. If you feel uncomfortable, if you're gasping for breath instead of breathing easily, if you think you'll drop with the next stride, you are pushing yourself too hard.

You're also overdoing it if you find that you're too tired to do anything else after you've worked out, if you lose so much weight that you look like a ghoul, or if you keep turning up with injuries related to your sport.

Generally, the more active you are, at a pace that's comfortable for you, the easier it should be for you to bounce back from a rugged workout, and the better you should look and feel.

As for what to do to get over the tension from a test or any other difficult or intense experience, ignore the advice above and head out for a long ride (or swim or run or walk), if that's what you feel like doing.

"You're late to class again! Where's your gymsuit? The penalty is five laps around the field. Get going!"

Adults who use exercise as punishment are making a mistake. Instead of helping you discover how good it feels to get yourself moving, they're turning motion into a humiliating experience. What kind of attitude do they expect you to have toward running when they use it to penalize you?

They'd be much smarter to make you sit still for a while. Then you'd start to think of doing nothing as punishment, and you'd realize how much better you feel when your body's in motion.

Fitness Is for Everyone

If you have a disabling condition or disease of any kind, you need exercise just as much as anyone else. Regardless of your problem, you can benefit from regular workouts. In some cases, diabetes and obesity, for example, exercise can actually help your condition improve.

Almost every day, people who have suffered paralysis, undergone an amputation, or been diagnosed with chronic disease break through athletic barriers, proving to others who share their condition that their problem is not necessarily an obstacle to general fitness.

How much and what kind of activity you take up depends on your particular condition and the kind of medication you may be taking for it. Your doctor should be in on any decision to start an exercise program, and should provide guidance and encouragement. If your doctor warns you against exercise, see if another doctor will offer you different advice.

One way to discover exercise options is to contact the local branch of the association established to provide information about your condition — the American Diabetes Association, the Epilepsy Society, the American Cancer Society, and so on. You could also talk with a physical therapist at a local hospital or rehabilitation center. Many people would rather not exercise than admit they need special help choosing a program. But the long-term problems that may develop from lack of motion could be much more painful than the few minutes of self-consciousness you may feel when you seek advice.

Be Confident

Some people let self-consciousness keep them from working out. They think that their physical difference makes them look or act funny, and that others will stare and laugh at them. Although there are insensitive people who might behave that way, they are relatively few compared with the many people who admire anyone willing to work at fitness. Keep in mind that the kinds of people who make fun are the ones with real disabilities. They aren't confident enough to feel good about themselves without putting down others.

Self-consciousness can also be a problem if you have to ask others for help while you're preparing to exercise — if you need assistance getting into the pool, for example, or climbing in or out of the shower.

Again, there are worse things than asking for help — getting weak and out of shape, to name two. Address people with confidence, and they will be glad to lend you a hand. Use a firm, self-assured voice when you respond to them, and your manner alone will let them know that you don't want pity and that you don't plan to answer any embarrassing questions they might ask. The stronger your voice in situations like this, the more you'll help others overcome their tendency to baby you or treat you with curiosity.

Surprise Symptoms

Another obstacle for some is unpredictable symptoms; with some diseases you never know when it might flare up. If you have diabetes, epilepsy, asthma, or arthritis, you may have to deal with this.

If this happens to you, and you're involved in a team sport, make sure that your coach and at least one teammate know how to recognize your symptoms and understand what to do if they show. You might feel weird about bringing it up, but you'd feel even worse if something happened and you had left them unprepared. If you tell them about it with confidence, in a way that lets them know you're not frightened or humiliated, they won't be scared or embarrassed, either.

It takes practice, patience, and familiarity with your body to get control of a chronic illness. You can help yourself by cooperating with your doctor, taking the appropriate medication in the proper amounts at the right times, and keeping your body as fit as you're able with an exercise program you truly enjoy.

Problem Parents

Parents of kids with disabilities or chronic diseases often react in one of two ways:

1. They become overprotective and warn you not to move a muscle. They feel responsible for everything that happens to you, and they're scared stiff of the "risks" they see in sports.

What they don't realize is that there are probably as many risks in getting little or no exercise. Strengthening and heart conditioning are important for everyone. Whatever limitations you might have because of your condition only get worse if you neglect your heart or let yourself become weak. Get your doctor to discuss exercise with you and your parents, so that all of you understand the benefits of a safe, appropriate athletic program.

2. They pretend there's no problem and push you into every conceivable form of athletics, just to prove to themselves that their kid is "okay." Maybe they say they're doing it to make you realize how capable and strong you are, but they may also be doing it to prove to themselves that they don't have a "defective" child.

Unless they've discussed it with your doctor, and she or he has agreed that you're too timid about exercise, your parents are not qualified to make those decisions for you. Only you and your doctor can determine what and how much you can and should be doing.

It's important for you as well as your family to remember that just because people with physical disabilities are participating in marathons, mountain-climbing expeditions, and other challenging athletic ventures, it doesn't mean that you have to push yourself to similar extremes. Just because you *can* do it, in other words, doesn't mean you *have* to do it. There's no reason why an exercise program for you should be any more demanding than one for others who don't have that extra challenge.

4

Stress

Stress affects your physical condition every bit as much as food and exercise. A combination of emotional and physical pressures, it can either help you deal with challenges and problems or make them many times worse.

Which effect stress has on you depends on how you handle it. And how you handle stress depends on being able to recognize it, knowing where it's coming from, and understanding your stress-management options so you can choose the best one for your situation. First things first. What is stress, and how do you know if you're under it?

Not for Adults Only

Try telling your average adult that you're under stress, and you're apt to get a lecture. You'll probably be told that you don't know the meaning of stress. "Wait until you've got bills to pay and a job to hold down. *Then* you'll know about stress!" Wrong. Everyone lives under some kind of stress. The stress you face at school, for example, is probably just as tough on you as the stress at work is on your parents. *You're under stress whenever the way you're feeling (emotionally) affects the way you're feeling (physically) and whenever the way you're feeling (physically) affects the way you're feeling (emotionally).*

Since stress involves your body *and* your mind, it can make you sick and drive you crazy at the same time — which is exactly what it will do if you don't learn to get it under control. But before you can begin to control it, you have to know what if feels like.

Here are some feelings that often come from stress. See if any of them apply to you.

- tired a lot of the time
- moods change for no reason
- cry over stupid things
- can't concentrate
- unenthusiastic about everything — no motivation to do anything
- fearful, but don't know what's frightening you
- can't sleep
- generally weak, feel that you have no strength
- shake a lot
- palms get sweaty
- head hurts
- have to run to the bathroom a lot

○ hungry no matter how much you eat
○ can't eat
○ accident-prone
○ have nightmares often

Some people come down with the same symptoms every time they're under stress — their palms always get sweaty, or they always have to run to the bathroom. Others react differently to each stressful situation. It's important to know how to respond to stress. Then you'll know when it's affecting you. From there, you'll be able to do something about it.

How Stress Works

Whenever you come up against something that upsets you in some way — scares you, frustrates you, angers you, makes you sad, nervous, or irritated — a part of your brain shoots stress hormones into your system. They trigger changes in the way your body is working. They can make your heart beat faster than normal. They can make your palms sweat. They can put a lump in your throat and knots in your stomach. They can make you hyper or they can make you drowsy. But believe it or not, although the sensations they cause are usually unpleasant, they can be very good for you.

The reason human beings have stress hormones in the first place is to warn us when we may be in trouble. Your heart starts racing when you're scared because it's preparing to help you speed away from danger. You'd need those extra heartbeats to push you on your way if you had to flee from something threatening.

The jumpy nerves you may have when a big test, an audition, or a recital is coming up can motivate you to spend extra time preparing for it. The sinking feeling you may get in your stomach when you're not prepared for class may get you to complete your homework assignments. And the discomfort you may feel when you break your parents' rules may help you obey them and stay out of trouble.

So Much for the Good Side of Stress

But then again, stress can be very bad for you. Anything that keeps your body from working normally for any length of time isn't good for it. If your stress responses are brief — just enough to warn you of danger — then they aren't much of a threat to your health. But when they go on and on, they can do a lot of harm.

Too much stress can make you feel lousy, give you a bad attitude, and make you a real drag to be with. But worst of all, it can make you unhappy and keep you from doing all you could do to have the kind of life you really want.

It's hard to keep stress responses under control. The reason is that stress works in a cycle, like this: Something upsets you, so the stress hormones start coming from your brain. The hormones throw off your system. Your system sends a message back to your brain, saying that it's in trouble. The message makes your brain even more upset, and so your brain sends out more stress hormones. They only upset your system more, and so it sends another distress message back to your brain. And how does your brain respond? By sending out more stress hormones, of course.

Learning how to break that cycle is the object of stress management. You can break the cycle by keeping your brain from sending out the stress hormones in the first place, or by keeping your body from reacting to the stress hormones from your brain.

But before you can do anything about stress, you have to know where it comes from.

Stressmakers:
People, Thoughts, and Situations
That May Be Stressful

Self-made Stress and What You Can Do about It

No one sets out to make her life stressful, so chances are you aren't aware of how you put yourself under stress.

No situation creates stress all by itself. It's how you think about the situation that makes it stressful.

For example, if you *think* that no one at your new school is going to like you, then heading off for your first day of school is bound to be stressful.

If you *think* that food will make you fat, then you're apt to feel under stress at mealtimes.

If you *think* that your family will forget about you when you go away from home by yourself, then leaving home may be a stressful experience.

What makes a situation stressful is different for everyone. You probably know at least one kid who loves to get up and perform for other people, whereas the thought of setting foot onstage might be enough to make you lose your lunch. The difference is this: she's thinking of it as her chance to show off, and you're thinking of it as everyone's chance to see what a jerk you can be.

Some of the Most Stressful Thoughts . . .

are thoughts that make you feel that you have no control over your life. They make you feel that things just happen to you for no good reason, that people are out to get you, and that all you can do is suffer helplessly.

Until you begin to believe that this is *your* life, thoughts like these will continue to put you under stress. True, as long as you're young a lot of other people will have power over you. But you can influence the way they use that power by expressing your own ideas, taking on more responsibility for yourself, and making an effort to understand why people do what they do.

See if any of the following thoughts seem familiar, then try to come up with ways to turn them around so that you're saying to yourself, "I *do* have an effect on the people around me." "I *can* make my life better." In other words, change the message so that you're giving yourself confidence instead of creating stress.

○ "It never pays to try hard, because nothing turns out right, anyway."
○ "I can't change the way my friends think, so I might as well go along with them."
○ "There's no way I can change my parents' minds about anything."
○ "What's going to happen is going to happen. There's not much I can do today to change what's going to happen tomorrow."
○ "When someone decides not to like me, there's nothing I can do to change her or his mind."
○ "There's no point in trying to get my way at home."

More Stressful Thoughts You'll Want to Avoid

As if that list isn't long enough, there are many other ways of thinking that can hurt you just as much. Again, as you read through the examples, consider how you might substitute a positive way of thinking for the stressful one.

Jumping to Big Conclusions:

> *You didn't get invited to the slumber party everyone's been talking about, and so you conclude that you'll never have any friends.*
> or
> *You get a poor grade on something you worked very hard at, and so you conclude that you're dumb.*

Thinking that you're dumb or that you can't possibly have any friends means that everywhere you go, you'll have to deal with the stress of worrying that people will view you in this way.

Actually, what you've done is reach some drastic conclusions from very skimpy evidence. The next time you get a bad break, don't assume that it's because there's something incurably wrong with you. Think about what's happened, and look for other explanations.

Being left out of one slumber party doesn't mean you're going to be a permanent outcast. Friends can be fickle. You may be "out" with them this week, and back "in" with them before long. Perhaps you'll never get along with that particular crowd, but that's hardly the end of your social life. Look for opportunities to meet new people and develop new friendships instead of imagining that you are an undesirable companion.

As for the bad grade, maybe you didn't understand what your teacher expected of you. Perhaps you did work hard but missed the point of the assignment. It's also possible that your work really wasn't as good as you thought it was. But that doesn't mean that everything you do will turn out badly, especially if you don't give up on yourself whenever you get a low grade.

Dwelling on the Worst:

You're pretty well liked at school, but you wouldn't exactly qualify as "Miss Popularity," and so you always worry about how many people aren't your friends instead of enjoying the ones who are.

Unless you want your life to be more stressful, there is absolutely no reason to think about disappointments and problems all of the time. Not that you should ignore the sore spots altogether — just don't let them blot out the good things that make you feel better about yourself.

Exaggerating:

You have a recital, game, or test coming up, and you decide that it's the Most Important Event of your life, and that your whole future happiness depends on how well you do.

Obviously, you can't be happy, calm, and confident if you think you're about to face the do-or-die moment of your life. Find ways to keep what's going on in perspective. Remember, even if you totally blow a test, performance, or game, you'll be alive afterward to make something of your next chance.

Being Paranoid:

> *You get a D on your test, and you swear it's because the teacher is out to get you.*
>
> **or**
>
> *You're in a competition and you don't even place, so you decide that the judges just didn't like the way you look.*

You can't have much confidence if you think that everyone is out to get you. You'd be lucky to get through life without having someone treat you unfairly. But it would be pretty strange if *everything* that happened to you was part of a plot by somebody else. Sometimes unfortunate things just happen, and usually you have more responsibility for what happens to you than anyone else.

The next time you're about to shift the blame, level with yourself. Did you really try your hardest? Even if you did, did you do as well as others in your class or at the competition? Instead of imagining the ways that others are trying to hurt you, think of ways to improve your work next time.

Being Envious:

> *You always compare yourself with other people. You're thrilled whenever you can prove that you're better than they are in some way,*

*but most of the time you're not sure that you
are, and so you're mostly dissatisfied with
yourself and angry at everyone who seems
prettier, smarter, or more popular than you
are.*

Envy is the worst. If you're busy envying people, and resenting them for being "better" than
you, it's almost impossible to find ways to make
yourself happier with them or with who you are.
When you're envious, you tend to make excuses
for yourself instead of making real efforts to be as
good as the people you envy, or to simply realize
that you already are.

Remember that hardly anyone is satisfied with
the way she is. The person you wish you were like
probably wishes she were like someone else. It's
apt to be an endless chain.

It also helps to realize that envy is pointless.
After all, you'll never *be* anybody but yourself. So
instead of wasting your time feeling envious and
down about yourself, realize that you can make
your life as good as anyone's — by discovering
what's really important to you. Once you know
what it is that you want, go for it.

Worrying about What Everyone Else Is Thinking:

*You're out with your father, who's wearing his
loud green trousers, and you're having a rotten time because you're sure that people are
thinking he's weird dressed like that.*
or
You never give your opinion before you've

*heard what your friends have to say, because
you're afraid they'll think you're dumb if your
thoughts happen to differ from theirs.*

How much fun can you have if you spend most
of the time worrying about what other people
think?

The only people worth caring about are the ones
who care about you. They're the ones who
wouldn't think about judging you (or your dad) by
your father's whacky taste in clothes. They're also
the ones who would be disappointed if you didn't
have your own opinions.

The next time you start working up stress over
what people are thinking, remember: Most people
are so busy worrying about how they come across
that they may not even notice whatever it is that
you're so concerned about. Even if they notice,
they simply won't care. Then, force yourself to
think of something else, preferably something
funny. As long as you've got something of your
own to think about, you can't be worrying about
what's going through other people's minds.

Other Stressmakers
And What You Can Do about Them

Others — parents, teachers, friends — put
stress on you when they expect you to do more
than you think you can do, or when they want you

to be different from the way you are or the way
you want to be.

There are four ways to deal with the stress you
may come under with parents, teachers, and
friends. Following this list you'll find a chart suggesting ways to use all four.

_____Four Ways to Handle Stress_____

1. **Get rid of what's causing the stress.**   This isn't
always the most practical idea, especially if a lot
of your stress comes from, let's say, your mother.
But other times it may be your best option. For
example, if you've found that you're too nervous
to sleep before each swim meet, and that you get
so worried about your performance that you don't
get any pleasure out of being in the pool during
practices or competitions, you might be better off
leaving the team for a noncompetitive athletic activity.

2. **Change your attitude toward what's causing the
stress.**   Decide that you're not going to let it get
to you anymore. For example, if your obnoxious
brother gets a kick out of hurling snakes at you,
resolve that you're not going to give him the pleasure of upsetting you. Get yourself to think of
snakes as truly marvelous creatures, and your
brother as a petty nuisance who doesn't deserve
to get a scream out of you.

3. **Face up to what's causing the stress until it's not
stressful anymore.**   Also known as the "sink or

swim" method, this involves plunging right into stressful situations, proving to yourself that you've got nothing to fear. For example, if you can't stand the thought of performing in front of other people, invite a few close friends or relatives to watch you. Gradually broaden your audience, perhaps asking your teacher to schedule a recital for you.

4. Deal with your reaction to the stress.   When stress makes you tense, get your body to relax. Do something physical to shake the stress from your system, or talk it out with a friend.

Family

When you can talk to your parents, when your household is loving and secure, then your family can help relieve a lot of the stress that you bring home from other places.

But home isn't heaven for everyone all of the time, and you can run into as many stressful situations there as you would anywhere else.

The following chart will help you understand how you can use the "Four Ways to Handle Stress" to deal with the stress you may find at home. It features some stressful situations common to many families: you'll probably find at least one familiar problem on it.

School

No matter how well you may be doing there, and no matter how much or how little you care about it, there are bound to be times when school creates stress for you. Here are some likely sources of stress at school, and some ways you might deal with them.

Teachers Who Are Out for Blood (Yours)

Some teachers like to keep the stress level high because they think a little pressure gets you to work harder. Other teachers like to keep the stress level high because they're bullies who get their kicks from making kids miserable. You can tell which is which, because the first kind usually eases up when you've done something well. The other kind never lets up, no matter how well you do.

You can deal with the first kind. Set aside a time to tell her or him that you might do better with a little more encouragement and a little less intimidation.

You can't do much about the second kind, but then again, neither can anyone else. Change your attitude; don't take it personally when she or he gets on your case — and don't give up on the subject that kind of teacher is teaching. Just because

Family Stress

	Get Rid of What's Causing the Stress
FIGHTS When your parents fight, there's the stress that disaster's going to strike any second, and the fear that you may lose one of them.	Try getting them to stop fighting (*before*, not during, their next one). Tell them you know they don't fight for the fun of it, but you wish they'd come up with a more peaceful way to work out their problems. If you can't get anywhere with them, ask a relative or a friend of theirs to bring it up for you.
RULES The rules your parents lay down for you can be stressful when they're only meant to let you know who's boss, and when they're much more strict than the ones your friends have to live with. Life can be pretty tough when you're the only one who has to be in by 9:00	Ask for a trial period with some of the rules repealed. Give your word that you won't go wild, you will get your chores and schoolwork done, and you won't turn into a degenerate. They may think that you won't respect their authority unless they smother you with it. You have to assure them that you'll respect them twice as much if they're willing to give you some trust. The flip side of that is that you have to handle that trust responsibly and live up to the promises you've made.

Change Your Attitude toward What's Causing the Stress	Face Up to What's Causing the Stress until It's Not Stressful Anymore	Deal with Your Reaction to the Stress
Face the fact that your parents have trouble getting along sometimes and comfort yourself by remembering that you're an innocent bystander. Try to understand how each of them feels instead of taking sides.	Just get used to it, if you can. Granted, this is harder than it sounds, and it may not work for you.	Take off on a bike ride or walk or run. Drop by to see a friend and talk it over. That'll get you out of the house and get what's going on in the house out of you. If you can't actually get away, try some relaxation exercises. Get on the phone with a friend or throw yourself into reading a book or writing a letter.
Look at it this way: a lot of those rules are meant to keep you from doing something dumb and dangerous. As unlikely as it may seem right now, your parents may be right when they tell you you'll be glad one day that they didn't let you have your way all of the time.	You may never enjoy living by the rules, but you may just make life more stressful for yourself by breaking them. Break them, and you have to live with the stressful fear of being caught and punished. Throwing things, screaming, threatening their life or yours, only gives them the satisfaction of knowing they're right to keep you under tight control.	Phone a friend and talk out your anger. Go for a run and take your aggression out on the pavement. Write a letter of protest to your parents, listen to music, try relaxation exercises.

	Get Rid of What's Causing the Stress
THEY EXPECT TOO MUCH They may tell you that they don't expect you to be perfect, but you know that if you're not, they'll say you didn't try. It's as if the only way you can prove you're trying is to be perfect	Explain that you appreciate their ambitions for you, but that the pressure isn't helping you achieve them. Cite specific examples, demonstrating how they pressure you and how it affects you. Also be ready to offer specific examples of how they could support you without the pressure.
THEY DON'T EXPECT ANYTHING While some of your friends can't get their parents off their backs, yours seem to have forgotten you were born.	Try telling your parents how you feel. Maybe they don't realize they're neglecting you. Letting them know might be enough to change things. Offer specific suggestions for things they can do to make you feel they care.

Change Your Attitude toward What's Causing the Stress	Face Up to What's Causing the Stress until It's Not Stressful Anymore	Deal with Your Reaction to the Stress
Decide that it's not worth worrying about what your parents want you to do. Maybe nothing short of bringing them riches and fame will make them happy. You *can* be expected to try your best, but it's unfair for anyone to expect you to make their dreams come true.	Try doing what they want you to do, and see what happens. Maybe you'll find that they're more easily pleased than you'd thought. Choose the one or two goals they have for you that are important to you, too, and work hard at them.	Shake off the stress with exercise, or talk it out with a friend or an adult who'll be more supportive than your parents have been. Talk to yourself, giving yourself the encouragement you'd like to hear from your folks.
One of the biggest myths going is that all parents love their children. Some just don't, and if yours happen to be among them, the last person you should blame is yourself. Your parents have problems; maybe they're too selfish, depressed, or angry to love anybody, even you. Maybe they don't love each other and are taking it out on you. Don't stop trying to be the best person you can be just because your parents don't seem to care. Plenty of other people will care.	There really isn't any way to apply this suggestion to this situation.	The effect of this kind of stress can be that you feel worthless. Find something to do — sports, volunteer work, extracurricular activities — that gives you a chance to prove your abilities and to get recognition for them.

	Get Rid of What's Causing the Stress
DIVORCE	This is one situation in which you can't get rid of the source of the stress. You can't do anything to keep the divorce from happening. In fact, you'll only make yourself feel a lot worse if you imagine you can.
DRUGS AND ALCOHOL There may be nothing harder to take than living with parents who have trouble with drugs or alcohol. Maybe they're unpredictable — all lovey-dovey one minute, then shrieking monsters the next. Maybe they've missed a lot of work, lost a job, or gotten nailed for drunk driving. Maybe they've hit you or each other.	Encourage your parent to get help from a hospital or rehabilitation program, like Alcoholics Anonymous. You might bring up the idea by saying you've noticed that drinking is making her or him unhappy; that other people have noticed and become concerned; that you're scared to be around her or him, and, as a last resort, you may go to court and ask to be allowed to live with a relative or someone else who could provide a safer, healthier home for you.

Change Your Attitude toward What's Causing the Stress	Face Up to What's Causing the Stress until It's Not Stressful Anymore	Deal with Your Reaction to the Stress
Instead of thinking that you're losing a parent, realize that you won't have to deal with the friction between your parents anymore. Life may be more peaceful.	Refuse to let either parent turn you against the other. Maybe you've already taken sides on your own for your own reasons. But if you feel that your parents are playing tug-of-war with you, remind them, "I don't have to hate him (or her) to love you."	Talk it out with friends, and keep yourself too busy to get caught up in your parents' problems. Every time you go to visit the parent you're not living with, you'll have to adjust to his or her new way of life. The best way to manage this stress may be to talk about how you feel, and get your parent to discuss his or her feelings, too.
Realize that your parents' problems are *their* problems and that you're not to blame for their condition. If they accuse you of causing them to drink or use drugs, they're lying.	Right away call Al-Anon Family Groups (listed in the white pages phone directory). Al-Anon is for kids who have to cope with parents with problems like yours. Call them now and find out how you can join. It won't change your parents' behavior, but it will help you learn to deal with the way they act, and provide you with a strong support system, too.	Get involved in activities that keep you occupied away from home. Develop a physical skill you can work on when stress builds up at home. Share your problems with a friend or an understanding adult.

the teacher is hard to take doesn't mean that the subject is dumb.

If you think you're being graded unfairly, take it up with your guidance counselor or the principal. Even if you can't get anything done about your grade, at least you're proving — to yourself as well as to the school — that you care enough about how well you're doing, and that you feel confident enough that you're doing your best, to challenge a teacher who's being unfair to you.

Teachers Who Like You

Even these teachers can put you under stress. They do it by making you feel that they'll be personally offended or disappointed if you don't do well all of the time.

Don't be fooled. They'll survive an occasional dip in your grades or performance. Adjust your attitude; you don't owe your teachers consistently perfect grades; you owe yourself consistently good effort.

If you have a teacher who's so easy on you that you're bored a good deal of the time, tell her or him that you think you'd be getting more out of school if more were expected of you. Make sure you specify that you're not after "busy work." Suggest getting projects meant for students in the next grade, or try to initiate projects you're especially interested in, then ask the teacher to work on them with you.

Tests

Tests are one of the more obvious sources of stress at school. Among the best ways to keep "test stress" from getting to you is to deal with the test by studying for it. Your stress level goes down when you know that you've spent time going over the material.

You can handle the effect stress has on you before a test by getting your body to relax. Breathing deeply and concentrating on something peaceful and pleasant will help you begin in a more productive way than if you let yourself panic and freeze.

Some attitudes that may help you approach the test are:

o "If I know it, I know it. If I don't, I don't."
o "If I don't do well, I can make up for it by doing something for extra credit, or by doing well on the next test. If all else fails, I can talk with the teacher and we can come up with a plan together. It's not hopeless!"
o "It's just another test."
o "No one ever died from taking a test."

You probably won't turn in all of your tension with the test paper, so let it out after school, by running, biking, walking, or dancing — whatever will help you spend that nervous energy.

Phys Ed

You're not alone if you dread gym class. Dealing with everything from the locker room to sports you would never in a million years choose to play can be decidedly loathsome.

But what if you have other reasons for hating phys ed? What if it's because everyone can see your fat jiggling when you're wearing your gym-suit? What if it's because you can't keep up when it's time to trot around the track?

Take a hint from your self-consciousness, and get yourself in shape. Gym class is not the problem . . . it just exposes your problem, which is excess weight. Instead of shying away from exercise, start taking it seriously. See a doctor as soon as possible to learn about other changes you can make so that gym class, and life in general, won't be so humilating for you anymore.

If it's just that you hate basketball, kickball, or whatever kind of ball they make you play . . . *relax*. Don't take it so seriously. Do the best you can. If your teammates try to make you take it seriously, fake it, reminding yourself meanwhile that they're the ones with the lousy attitudes, making a big deal out of a simple game.

It also helps if you're good at another sport outside phys ed. You won't get down on yourself for being the world's worst volleyball player if you know you could outlast most people on a bicycle trip, for example.

Strange as it may seem if you really hate phys ed, you *can* get something out of it. You can get a

chance to work out some of the tension that's
built up during the day. When it's time to do exercises, really *do* them. If you're angry or upset
about something, think about it while you're in
motion, and you might find that the anger or
worry isn't as intense when you're through.

Friends

At times, friends can be your best defense
against stress. At other times, they only add to it.

Most of the things that your friends do that
bother you start with something that bothers them.
They're insecure, lonely, dissatisfied with themselves, angry, or bored.

Try to figure out why your friends act the way
they do. Once you know what's really going on
with them, they may not get to you so much anymore. Besides, you'll be able to help them feel
better about themselves, which is one of the things
friends are for.

Make a list of the things your friends do that
annoy you. Then go over the list and try to think
of reasons (besides deliberately driving you crazy)
for their behavior.

Some reasons might be:

○ They want attention.
○ They want sympathy.
○ They want approval because they're not sure
    of themselves.
○ They want to feel like they belong.

Now see if you recognize any of these situations:

One of my friends is always pulling off my hat or scarf, or grabbing food from me while I'm eating.

Maybe she wants your attentions and thinks that the only way to get it is by being obnoxious. Instead of flaring up at her, tell her she shouldn't be so desperate for attention, that it's only ruining her chances for having any attention at all.

Maybe she's upset about something and won't feel better until you're upset, too. Again, try not to blow up — that's what she expects. Try to keep cool long enough to ask her what's bothering her, and why she feels she has to act that way to get your attention. Calmly tell her that you don't like being around her when she's like this, and you won't stick with her if she keeps it up.

One of my friends is always bragging.

Maybe she doesn't really feel very good about herself and brags to try to get other people to tell her she's terrific. In other words, she's bragging because she's insecure — not because she's confident. If that's so, just remind yourself of this and remind her that you like her just the way she is.

Maybe she *isn't* bragging. Maybe she's just telling you about something she's done. It may sound like bragging to you if you haven't done anything you're as proud of, or if you tend to compare yourself with her. If that's so, you have to start feeling better about yourself before you can stop being annoyed by her.

"One of my friends spreads my secrets all over town."

This is often another sign of insecurity. Friends who do this think that the only way to make new friends is to impress them by spreading gossip about others. You only make this worse if you start some kind of war over it, using your friend's secrets to get back at her for spreading yours.

The best thing you can do is to work on your attitude. Realize that she's not necessarily doing this to hurt you (even though it does hurt). She's doing it to help herself. Once you understand this, you may be able to help her find other ways to deal with her insecurity.

Tell her that other people — you, for one — will like her even more if they can trust her. Tell her that even though you don't like to have your secrets spread all over town, she's the one who's likely to end up worse off — no one will want to tell her anything once they find out about her big mouth. People would be more apt to like her if she'd just be who she is, without trying to "use" her other friends.

When They Try to Make Their Problems Your Problems

Some of your friends may deal with their problems in ways that make them much worse. Friends who start drinking, doing drugs, skipping school, shop-lifting, and running away may think they're doing it for fun. They may try to get you to go along for a "good time."

Your friend thinks she's having fun because she can't stand to face what's going on in her life and is trying to get away from her problems. But she's really just making more trouble for herself.

These kinds of escapes *never* work. For one thing, escapes don't get rid of the problems; they just avoid them for a while. Also, you run the risk of doing damage to yourself and others and of being caught if you're doing something illegal.

Your friend may think she's too smart for that, but there've been millions of people — many of them far smarter than your friend — who have learned about this the hard way: by damaging their bodies and brains from alcohol and drugs; by getting caught and punished for skipping school; and by finding they still have to face the problems they were trying to escape in the first place.

Your friend may want you to go along because she's not so sure about what she's doing. She may think that having you by her side makes it okay.

The only way you can help her make things okay is to help her figure out what she's trying to escape and to encourage her to find some way to deal with it. Offer to go with her to see a family counselor if she's having trouble at home; a doctor if her problems have to do with sex or her body; a teacher or counselor if her trouble is at school.

If you can't get her to begin coping with her problems in a positive way, don't make a bad thing worse by doing what she wants you to do. An important part of growing up is recognizing

when it's time to make an independent decision,
even if it means cutting loose from a friendship.

When Your Friends Care about Nothing But Boys, and Make Having a Boyfriend Seem Like the Most Important Thing in the World

Some of the more stressful problems with friends
begin when they make you feel you're supposed to
have a boyfriend. Friends alone don't make you
feel that way. They just echo a message you get
from movies, television shows, songs, and advertisements, and that message is: you're really missing out if you're not attached to someone.

Romantic relationships are very important.
There's no doubt that life would be dreary without
them. But a romantic relationship and someone to
share it with are not things you can go out and get
just because you feel you ought to have them.
What does it mean to have a boyfriend, anyway?
And what makes the difference between a boyfriend and any other friend?

For some of your friends, the only difference
may be that a boyfriend is someone you can get
physical with. But sometimes the awkwardness
and self-consciousness they may feel once they
cross the line from being friends to being boyfriend and girlfriend can keep them from being as

close as they were when they were "just friends," or as close to each other as they are to their other friends. Relationships between boys and girls don't necessarily improve when they decide to become "more than friends," especially if they haven't been friends very long.

The best romantic relationships develop over time between people who have gotten to know and like each other as friends. But many girls are so concerned about having a boyfriend that they don't bother with the time and friendship needed to make the relationship work. That's why you'll find at least some of your friends going out with lots of guys, but never feeling close to any of them.

If you're uncomfortable with the pressure to have a boyfriend, try to escape it by getting active in something — volunteer work, an art program, music, athletics — that doesn't involve your boy-minded friends. You may have found that your friends spent so much time and effort on boys that they've given up some of the interests they used to have. What they don't realize is that they'll end up with many more friends in the long run — including boyfriends — if they develop interests and abilities now that make them interesting, worthwhile companions.

What if the pressure is affecting the relationships you already have? It can be hard to keep friendships with boys when everyone seems to expect that all relationships between boys and girls will become romantic. You can come under a lot of stress if you discover that a guy you're friendly with is attracted to you, especially if you don't want to get closer to him than the table you share when you're at the library together. The best way to handle that stress is to deal with it directly. Tell him you're not comfortable with the idea of changing your relationship with him right now. Unless you deal with the situation honestly, it, and the stress it causes, will go on and on.

You can put yourself under a lot of stress if you're the one trying to change the relationship, especially if all you want from the change is to "have a boyfriend" so you can feel you belong. If the boy you have in mind doesn't want to go along with you, you may feel rejected and let down.

Remember: just because friendships *can* turn into romances doesn't mean they *have* to or that they always will. Keep in mind that often boys your age aren't as interested in the kind of relationship you may want. They will be, eventually. Meanwhile, do your best to hold onto and build your friendships. Just waiting for romance to roll around can be dull and depressing.

Any relationship that lets you feel trust and closeness is one worth keeping as it is. Don't let anyone pressure you into changing valuable relationships just so you can become the way they think you should be. Good relationships should help you deal with stress, not create more of it — that goes for romantic relationships as well as friendships.

Do-It-Yourself Stress Management

Now that you've gone over examples showing you how you can handle stress from various specific sources, try to apply what you've learned to other stressful situations in your life.

○ Figure out what's causing the stress.
○ Go over the "Four Ways to Handle Stress" and figure out which approach would be best for you. (You might even combine a few of them.)
○ Write out a plan of action, the changes you'll make and the steps you'll take to handle the stress.
○ Put that plan into action immediately.

What's Putting Me under Stress ____and What I Can Do about It____

1. What's putting stress on me: _____

_____ .

2. What I can do about it:
   a. Get rid of it (how?)
   b. Face up to it (how?)
   c. Change my attitude toward it (how?)
   d. Deal with how it makes me feel (how?)

_____*More Stressmakers*_____

Criticism

Maybe there's no difference to you between being criticized and being clobbered over the head. Both hurt, and both can make you a little reluctant to get yourself into a situation where it can happen again.

The trick to coming out on top of things is *not* managing to get by without criticism. The only way to avoid criticism is to avoid doing anything at all. The trick is knowing what to do with the criticism you get.

Criticism will be less stressful, and even helpful, if you:

- ○ Remind yourself that your objective is to do better. In order to do that, you need to know what you're doing wrong.
- ○ Ask your critics to make specific comments; don't let them get away with saying your work (your performance, your clothing, whatever) stinks. Tell them you won't have any reason to trust what they say unless they can explain themselves.
- ○ Discuss the criticism. Ask questions. Suggest some ideas you have for doing things better, and encourage them to help with more.

Wanting Success

Everyone wants success. But hardly anyone agrees about what it is. If your idea of success is to be rich, famous, beautiful, and to have whatever you want whenever you want it, you might have a problem.

That's not the kind of success you come by every day — even on a good day. With that kind of goal, the most you could expect is a lot of frustration and, along with that, a lot of stress.

There's nothing wrong with having big goals and big ambitions unless they make you so dissatisfied with what you've got that you're unhappy and restless most of the time. Success doesn't have to mean "perfection." It doesn't have to mean getting your life story in *People* magazine. It can mean whatever you want it to mean.

Boredom

Believe it or not, boredom is stressful. When you've got nothing else to do, you have plenty of time to sit around thinking how rotten it is that you have nothing to do. Boredom makes you dwell on your problems, whereas being active allows you to get your mind onto more interesting and uplifting things.

Discover what your interests are and do something about them. Find things to do that involve other people. The more you get involved with other people's lives, the less you'll mull over what's wrong with your own.

Success without Stress

Here are two ways to look at success. One way is stressful, the other is not.

Goal	Stress-free Idea of Success	Stressful Idea
a "successful" body	has plenty of energy for everything you want to do; the clothes you like come in your size, and you can see your toes when you're standing up	could model this year's skimpiest swimsuits
"success" at school	knowing that you're learning; feeling your thoughts and ideas develop; getting along well with at least one teacher	getting all A's. Teachers adore you.
"success" at sports	enjoying the time you spend playing; knowing that your skills are improving, and feeling yourself getting stronger	winning; making varsity
a "successful" social life	having a few really close friends; being friends with some boys	having hundreds of friends and a serious boyfriend
a "successful" family life	knowing there is room for mistakes and disagreements; being able to talk openly with each other	no fights, ever; always getting your way

You can get over boredom by:

○ Talking to people about what they do to keep busy. Ask if you can go along to their next meeting or lesson, just to see if you want to get involved in what they're doing.
○ Dropping by the nearest Girls' Club or Y. Not only is there a lot going on, but you'll get to meet kids from other schools, who may turn out to be better friends than the ones you have now.
○ Getting involved in school activities. Maybe you're shy about it because it seems as if certain groups already run everything. It may not be easy to break in, but once you prove you've got something to offer, like hard work, enthusiasm, and ideas, they won't want to let you go.
○ Doing volunteer work in the community. By reaching out to help others at a local hospital, day-care center, ecology project, or youth recreational program, you can eliminate boredom while finding out how satisfying it is to make a real contribution to others.

Disorganization

When everything around you is in chaos, just finding a pencil to do your homework can be stressful. When you're disorganized, you can have trouble remembering when your homework assignments are due, which ones are completed, and which ones you have yet to begin. In other words, disorganization can lead to trouble, which can only lead to more stress.

Organize Your Room.   Arrange things according to a sensible plan, so you don't have to search unlikely places for items that should be right on your desk, in your closet, or wherever. Take the time to put things where they belong, and you'll save time later trying to remember where you put them.

Organize Your Time.   Get a calendar and write down everything that's coming up: when an assignment is due, when you're supposed to take off on vacation, when you're going to be baby-sitting, and so forth. Once you can see when things are going to happen, you won't feel as if everything catches you by surprise.

Organize Your Homework.   Before you jump into an assignment, figure out which books you'll need, then flip through them and put markers in the sections you'll be using. This way you won't have to take your mind off your work to mess with details like finding the right place in the right book.

If an assignment is due in one week, figure out how much work you'll have to do each day in order to get it in on time. If it's a book report, for example, plan to read enough chapters each day to finish the book in three or four days. Plan to spend one day outlining your report, another writing the rough draft, and another writing the final draft.

You can handle a research paper in pretty much

the same way — spend the first few days reading and taking notes, and the rest outlining and writing.

Write down your work schedule as soon as you get the assignment, so you won't foul yourself up by letting research days spill into writing days.

Worry

Whenever you worry, no matter what it's about — friends, problems at home, trouble at school — you're usually worrying for the same basic reason: you feel that things are going wrong, and there's nothing you can do about it.

But worrying is like poisoning yourself. When you just keep running the same old problem through your head over and over, you're stuffing your system with stress. Instead of worrying about a problem, *find a way to deal with it* or *do something to get it off your mind.*

Relax

So far, everything you've read has dealt with using thoughts, attitudes, and actions to handle stress. But what if you can't help feeling stressed? When you're on your way to your first day at a new school, for example, or waiting backstage for your turn to perform, or anticipating the start of a big game.

Something to Do When You Feel Like Worrying

Write down three things that you could do to *actually improve* the situation you're worrying about. What could you *do* to make things better?

1. _____

2. _____

3. _____

Write down three things that could be much worse than what you're worrying about. What could be going wrong that would upset you even more?

1. _____

2. _____

3. _____

Write down three things you could do to get your mind off what's worrying you. What could you *do* to forget about it for awhile?

1. _____

2. _____

3. _____

At those times, you can handle the stress by getting your body to relax.

Learning to relax is like learning a new sport. It's not something that comes automatically; it takes practice and skill. What *does* come automatically is the opposite of relaxation: tension.

Tension is all of the unpleasant sensations you have when you're under stress: headaches, stomachaches, heavy perspiration, and so forth. When you get yourself to relax, the tension vanishes. Not only that . . . relaxation helps you shake off some of the stress that caused the tension in the first place.

Before you can learn how to relax, you have to be aware of the difference between how you feel when you're relaxed and when you're tense. Here's how:

1. Lie on your back on the floor.
2. Close your eyes.
3. Picture yourself in the most nerve-wracking situation you can imagine.
4. With this idea in mind, start clenching your teeth and your fists. Point your toes as hard as you can, and scrunch up your shoulders.
5. Add more tension by imagining some guy you like walking in and finding you like this.

You are now tense.
Now begin to relax.

1. Start taking a deep breath — a long, slow one.
2. As you breathe, start to let go — stop

clenching your fists, let your toes go limp, wriggle and lower your shoulders.

3. While you're doing this, change the picture in your mind. Go from the most upsetting

Picture This

You can prepare for stressful situations ahead of time by picturing yourself making it through them.

Athletes do it all the time — instead of worrying about whether or not they're going to be able to pull off a successful routine, match, or whatever, they imagine themselves doing it from start to finish. They relax, and then watch themselves play or perform. They set up sticky situations, and then see themselves get by them. They play the game, run the race, or perform the routine over and over — perfect every time.

When they're finally "on" for real, they're confident because they feel like they've done it already a hundred times.

This doesn't work only for athletes. Try it the next time you have to do something that's usually petrifying. Picture what you'd do or say to make everything turn out the way you want it to. Use this technique:

Before tryouts for band, a team, cheerleading, a play
Before you meet with a teacher about your grades
Before an interview to get into a new school
Before you leave home for school, camp, or a long visit

_____ (*your own idea*)

_____ (*your own idea*)

thought to the most comforting — a happy
memory, a favorite place, a favorite person.
4. Keep breathing deeply while you have this
thought in mind.

Obviously, the next time you get up to give an
oral report or do something equally stressful,
you're not going to dive onto the floor and relax in
this way.

But now that you know how it feels to be relaxed, you can let out your tension while sitting or
standing, looking perfectly normal.

Depression

Even though you often hear people link depression with suicide, depression doesn't always make
you feel like killing yourself. It doesn't even always make you feel sad. It can just make you feel
tired all the time, or make you feel that you're not
interested in anything — even things you used to
get excited about.

Probably the most common feeling that comes
with depression is the feeling that you don't care
about what's happening in your life, or about
doing anything to make it better. Everyone feels
like that from time to time, but if you feel that
way week after week, it's a safe bet that you're
depressed and that you need some help to get
over it.

You can start with someone you feel close to. An adult might be better able to help you, simply because most have had more experience with emotions than someone your own age. Bring it up with one of your parents, or discuss it with a teacher you trust. Maybe the parents of one of your friends can help.

If you don't think any of those options would work, try your doctor. Just call and describe how you've been feeling. Maybe he or she will want to see you about it, or perhaps you'll be referred to another doctor who has more experience with problems like yours.

If you don't like that idea, check the "Community Services" section at the front of the white pages phone directory, and find the number of the Mental Health Association. They'll tell you where you can go for low-cost or free help.

Even if you're not feeling suicidal, the suicide prevention hotline in your area (also listed at the front of your phonebook) can help you deal with your depression.

Whichever call you decide to make — to your doctor, your local mental health association, or the suicide prevention hotline — make it now. Nobody can help you until they know that you need them.

Do You Have Blue Genes?

Doctors are beginning to find that some kinds of depression run in families, the way green eyes or freckles might. These people get depressed because some part of their brain or nervous system isn't working as it should . . . and that means their depression can be controlled or cured, like many physical illnesses, which is very hopeful news.

If you've been having problems with depression, try to find out if anyone in your family has ever had a mental illness. Has anyone committed suicide? Spent time in a psychiatric hospital? Had trouble with drugs or alcohol? Any of those things might — but does not by any means have to — indicate that you have inherited a tendency to get depressed.

You might have trouble getting the information you need; few families are dying to discuss their more "disturbed" members. Maybe eventually people will realize that mental illness has a lot in common with other kinds of disease, and that it isn't the patient's fault. Once that happens, they won't be ashamed to talk about it anymore.

For now, try to convince someone in your family that you have a right to that information because it may be useful if you ever need help with an emotional problem. Ask around until you find someone who's willing to talk. Once you do, keep in mind that it's enough to know that someone has suffered severe depression. Prying for details is an unfair invasion of privacy.

If You Ever Think of Suicide

Life can be so disappointing, unfair, and difficult that you'd have to be either very lucky or very crazy to be happy all of the time. But there's a big difference between being bummed for a while and being depressed enough to want to do yourself in.

Suicide *will* put an end to your problems. Trouble is, you won't be around to know that your problems are gone. All of the things you hate about your life will be over with. But you won't be here to feel good about it.

No Pity

Sometimes it seems that suicide would be an effective way to make everyone feel sorry for kicking you around, putting you down, or ignoring you. But it's important to realize that you'll never know whether it really worked out that way . . . you won't be at your funeral to count the tears. Also, it's not unusual for the people who get left behind to resent the person who killed herself. They sense that their dead friend or relative was trying to make them feel guilty, and they often do whatever they can to forget all about it.

Not for the Brave

Another thing that can make suicide appealing to some people is the way it's been made to seem like a "noble" or "artistic" thing to do. In drama, poetry, music, and biographies of some famous people, individuals who have committed suicide have been glorified as "brave" or "extraordinarily sensitive."

But, looking at it another way, it takes more
courage to ask for help than it does to give up on
yourself and the idea of changing your life. Also,
being sensitive and aware of your feelings can help
enrich your life, but when your sensitivity becomes so extreme that you withdraw from others,
it's no longer a good thing.

The First Thing
to Do . . .

when the idea of killing yourself seems like the
best or only way to deal with your problems is to
tell someone exactly how you feel. That may not
seem like practical advice. After all, you might be
feeling suicidal *because* you don't have anyone to
talk to. In that case, call the suicide-prevention
hotline in your area. Just about every community
has one — look under "Hotlines" in the "Community Services" section of your white pages tele-
phone directory. You won't have to give your
name, and you can call as often as you want and
talk for as long as you'd like to. Many of the people answering the phones will have had similar
feelings and will be able to understand yours.

If you do bring it up with friends or relatives
and they don't seem to take you seriously, don't
assume that they don't care. They're probably just
not sure how to handle it. They might have diffi-
culty believing you. Also, they might assume that
if they ignore you, you'll forget about it. Their
seeming lack of concern might prompt you to

make a suicide attempt, just to try to convince them that you mean business. If so, consider the possibility that your attempt could leave you *much worse off* than you are right now. Lots of people who've made attempts have ended up with brain damage, hideous scars, and other serious injuries.

Timely Help

What you need is someone who will take you seriously *before* you try something drastic. If you don't know anyone like that — if none of your family, friends, teachers, friends' parents, or relatives seems to want to understand how you're feeling — then, again, call the suicide-prevention hotline in your community. They won't be surprised to hear from you . . . the only reason they're there is to offer support to people who have problems like yours.

5
Growing Healthy, Staying Healthy

Other Things to Consider

Smoking

The trick to making a good decision about anything is to think out the pros and cons of all sides very carefully before you choose. Most truly dumb decisions are made on the spur of the moment, without a real thought, often to impress someone else or prove something to parents.

Deciding whether or not to smoke is no different. You add up the pros and cons, see which side has more going for it, then choose whichever comes out ahead.

If you're having trouble making choices about smoking, here's a list of cons for starters. Add any pros you can think of, then go ahead and decide.

○ Smoking stinks. Smoke particles cling to the lining of your mouth and tongue, where even breath mints can't get at them. If you smoke, your breath is bound to be awful.

   Smoke clings to your clothing, too. You may end up paying a hefty dry cleaning bill if your mother sniffs out your smoke-scented clothes.

○ Smoking stains your teeth and ruins your smile. You just might end up learning this the hard way, if your dentist tells your mother you've got these "funny yellow stains, usually associated with cigarette smoking."

○ Smoking ruins your skin. The crud from the smoke makes your skin grimy; you can't keep it clean enough to prevent zits. Also, the smoke drains color from your complexion and keeps perfume from sinking into your skin (which it must do in order to give off scent). Most models (including those who pose for cigarette ads) know this and don't smoke.

○ Smoking is becoming less popular. You're more likely to run into people who object to cigarette smoke and who won't mind telling you that smokers are dumb to risk their health and waste their money.

○ Worst of all, smoking wrecks your health, not only by giving you a greater chance of lung cancer or heart disease later on, but by damaging your system right now. It's hard to keep yourself in shape once you take up smoking, because your muscles can't get the oxygen they need in order to make it through a good workout. Also, you can't work out for long without losing your breath.

What's more, smoking destroys a lot of the nutrients that should be nourishing your skin, hair, and bones. Vitamin C can't stand up to cigarettes, so people who smoke come down with more colds each year than people who don't.

Drinking

When teachers and parents warn you about drinking, they usually give you some dull statistics — how many kids are killed or injured in drinking-related accidents every day (50 killed, 200 badly hurt), and how many teenagers graduate high school with drinking problems (2 out of 5 boys, and 1 out of 5 girls).

Beer commercials and liquor ads, though, don't bother with boring statistics. They make drinking look like pure fun. It's much easier to relate to those ads than to a bunch of hard-luck numbers.

You have to decide for yourself what the real story is. But to do that, you have to know what drinking can do to you.

○ Drinking makes you feel together even when you're totally out of control. That's why you're more likely to fall or have some other kind of accident when you're drunk.

So what? You break a few bones and get to brag about how smashed you were when it happened.

But what if the injuries are more serious than that? There's no way to predict what kind of damage you'd do to yourself or to others. You might burn your face or scar it some other way. You could suffer brain damage. Injuries like those are nothing to brag about.

○ Drinking makes you feel cool when you're acting like a jerk. Next time your friends get together to drink, stay straight and watch. Chances are you'll be disgusted by how idiotic they look.

○ Drinking can make you reckless; you may get relaxed enough to do or say things you'll later regret.

○ You can lose your memory. It's pretty embarrassing to have someone else tell you what a riot you were last night — especially if you don't think that what you supposedly did was so funny.

○ Chances are you'll have a hangover. If you've ever wanted to spend a day throwing up and nursing a throbbing head, here's your chance.

___Dumb Reasons to Start Drinking___

To Feel Grown-up.   Adults who do a lot of drinking are trying to forget that they are adults with responsibilities. In other words, they're trying to be like children. Imitating childish adults shouldn't make you feel grown-up.

Because You're Bored.   Anything that's easy gets boring after a while. Drinking will get dull, too. Then what'll you do? Drink more? And when that gets boring, will you drink even more? That's exactly how many teenagers develop drinking problems; drinking starts to lose its thrill, so they need more and more alcohol to enjoy themselves. They lose their ability to find pleasure in any other way, and before long, they've lost their health, their chance to do well in school, and the confidence of their friends and family.

To Forget Your Problems.   Your problems will be there when you sober up, so what's the point?

To Be Accepted.   Friendships that are based on drinking don't last long. They fall apart for the same reason that drinking gets boring — it's just the same thing over and over again. Those relationships have nowhere to go. When you build friendships around a sport or another activity, your relationships can grow. You can work at achieving something together, which is a much stronger basis for friendship than sharing a six-pack or so.

Drugs

Like alcohol — which is a drug — other drugs can corrode your memory, destroy your judgment, and make it impossible to feel good without them.

Even drugs like marijuana and cocaine that aren't physically addictive (meaning that your body needs the drug in order to function), can make you emotionally dependent. Once you become used to the sense of well-being you may get from dope or cocaine, you may find it harder and harder to cope with normal, everyday ups and downs.

Marijuana smoke does a worse job on your body than cigarette smoke. It eats away at the lungs and stomach and can cause hormones to go berserk, possibly affecting sexual development. Guys who've used a lot of dope have been known to develop breasts large enough to require surgical removal. Anything that can cause something that bizarre to happen can hardly be considered harmless.

People snort cocaine or use drugs made from it, like crack, because it makes them feel energetic and able to handle their problems. But when they discover what else it does, many of them wish they had never touched the stuff. They discover that it costs a lot of money to get as much as they want, and that they may have to steal to support their habit. They also find out that it makes their nose run and bleed. Worst of all, cocaine can kill you — even the very first time you try it.

One last thing to keep in mind before you go partying with your friends. Teenagers are the largest source of transplant organs in the country. That means that more teenagers die suddenly in accidents than any other members of the population, leaving healthy organs that could have kept them going for many more years.

To give yourself the best chance to develop a sharp mind and a strong body, don't do drugs of any kind.

Saying No to Cigarettes, Alcohol, and Drugs

Adults call it "peer pressure," but to you, it's just going along with what all of your friends are doing. The way it usually works is that you're out with your friends, and they decide it would be really fun or really cool to do something that everyone knows she's not supposed to do: smoke, drink, do dope, or drive — when you've got no right to be on the road. And *you* either go along or look like a geek.

There's bound to be trouble for you whether you go along or not. If you *do* go along with the others, you may get caught and punished. Worse, you may get hurt. If you *don't* go along with them, you could end up feeling left out.

What you need is a way to handle those situations that prevents either consequence.

The ideal way out of peer pressure is to tell your friends that you don't want to smoke, drink, or use drugs. It's not easy to announce this to the whole group at once, so you might try explaining yourself to your friends one at a time. Some of them are bound to understand and will stick with you. Others might need the comfort they get from going along with the crowd too much to understand and appreciate what you're doing. They might give you a hard time and try to make you feel left out. That's when you need your other friends, your family, or teachers to support you and remind you that you don't have to do stupid, dangerous things to have good friendships and love. In fact, really good friends will want you to do things that keep you healthy and happy — not things that could do you harm or get you into trouble.

When You Can't Say No

Still, there may be times when it seems impossible to tell your friends straight out that you don't want to go along with what they're doing. At those times you have to be able to say something else to keep from giving in to pressure to do something you don't want to do. Here are some ideas.

Keep in mind that these are meant only as temporary solutions. The sooner you can tell your friends that you don't want to go along with everything they do, the better off you'll be. But unless you have the confidence to do that right now, you may want to try some of these suggestions until you do.

Put Off Your Friends without Putting Them Down

You're at a sleepover, and everyone's staying in the rec room, where the liquor cabinet happens to be. Bottles start making their way around, but you're not interested. When one of your friends passes one to you, you say:

"Thanks, I'd better not. This stuff makes me really sick. If I barf on your rug, you'll get caught for sure."

This works because you're excusing yourself without criticizing your friends. At the same time, you're gently dropping the reminder that drinking can make them sick, too. Also, you're acting as if you're doing your friends a favor by refusing to drink; they probably won't push you to do something that might get them caught.

You're walking home from school with some friends and one of them pulls out a pack of cigarettes. You don't want to smoke. But you don't want them to make you feel like a drip, either. So you say:

"I really don't feel like it now, thanks."

If they keep after you, offering again and again, tell them the truth — that you don't want to start smoking, now or ever. Tell them you thought they'd get the hint when you kept putting them off, and you hope they'll stop asking you because it makes you uncomfortable to have to say no.

You're at your friend's house and her parents aren't home. They've stocked the refrigerator with beer for a big party later in the week. Your friend takes one and says you can help yourself. Getting buzzed wasn't on the list of things you wanted to do that day, so you say:

"Nah, I'd rather have iced tea."

This works because you're not just rejecting her idea, you're coming up with a positive alternative. *And* when you say you'd prefer iced tea (or milk, or juice, or water), you're letting her know that alcohol isn't a big deal for you. She thinks she's being cool by offering you that beer; you're gently letting her know that, as far as you're concerned, she's not.

You're at the library studying with some friends, and they decide to go out back and get high. You feel funny about telling them you just don't want to do drugs, so you play up your need to get your homework done, and say:

"I'm in real trouble in Keating's class. He said he'll flunk me if I screw up on this assignment."

Later, when you have time to explain yourself, you can let them know that you're not about to get involved with drugs. The sooner, the better, so you won't find yourself having to make up excuses again.

An important part of growing up is deciding what's important to you, and how you're going to act and what you're going to do with your body. Growing up involves thinking for yourself, and taking responsibility for your actions — even if it means leaving behind certain friends who aren't willing to be as responsible or independent.

Making decisions that go against your friends can make life lonely for a while. But before long you'll discover that the rewards — good health, self-confidence, and better friendships — are worth all of the trouble you went through to get them.

Self-Care during Your Period

From Cramps to Crankiness: Dealing with Common Preperiod Complaints

Some women handle all of the changes in their bodies each month without feeling a thing. Others swell up, get headaches, have cramps, feel crabby, or pig out. Still others feel just fine one month, and miserable the next.

Menstrual Hygiene

While you're menstruating, you have to pay extra attention to hygiene (cleanliness) and fitness.

Do	Don't
Shower every day. Menstrual fluid doesn't have an odor of its own, but it starts to smell when it mingles with bacteria on your skin. The cleaner you keep yourself, the less bacteria — and less odor — there'll be.	Waste money on "feminine hygiene deodorants." If you bathe daily, you just don't need them.
Experiment with different brands of pads and tampons until you find the one that's most comfortable for you.	Use "super absorbency" tampons. You run a higher risk of getting "toxic shock" with them because they make it easier for the wrong kind of bacteria to grow. Toxic shock is an infection that can cause everything from simple vomiting and diarrhea to death. Why take the risk? It can be avoided by using regular absorbency tampons, changing them often, and switching back and forth beween tampons and pads.
Exercise as much as usual. Unless you're gravely ill, you'll never lose enough blood during your period to make you feel weaker. Women have participated in Olympic competitions while menstruating (including swimming). Exercise, in fact, will help prevent and relieve cramps.	

The swelling, cramps, and other uncomfortable symptoms that some women experience before or during menstruation are commonly known as PMS — pre (meaning before) menstrual syndrome (meaning a group of symptoms or problems). It's called *pre*menstrual syndrome because most of the discomfort occurs before the period actually starts.

Blame It on Hormones

PMS strikes when hormones get out of whack. Instead of doing only what they're supposed to (strengthening the wall of your uterus, for example), they do too many other things. Some of them keep salt from leaving your system. The extra salt makes your body hold in too much water, and the extra water makes you swell up. Sometimes the hormones keep your body from using sugar properly and end up making you crave sweets. Hormones can also help produce substances that cause cramps just below your stomach.

What You Can Do

No one knows how to control hormones, but most doctors believe that they are affected by the way you think and feel. There's some evidence that girls and women who worry about getting PMS may actually bring it on themselves. So it could be that one way to avoid it is not to think about it. Another way is to exercise often and eat a well-balanced diet. The hormones that arrive just before menstruation tend to behave better in a body that's in good condition all month long.

A Few Practical Suggestions

Swelling: If your jeans, shoes, or rings get a little snug right around your period, lay off salty foods for about two weeks before your next period. Also, drink lots of plain water. As long as you're not taking in more salt, the fresh water will help flush out the water that is making you swell. Don't take water pills. They can make you dangerously dehydrated.

Cramps: The best cure is prevention. Exercising all month long can really help. If you still get cramps, pile some books on the floor until you've made a stack about a foot high. Lie flat on your back with your feet on the books. Stay there for ten minutes or so. If that doesn't work, take a plain aspirin. *Don't* take water pills. Menstrual cramps have nothing to do with extra water, even though the ads for those pills may tell you otherwise.

Headaches: Again, hold the salt. The pain may come from water building up in your head. Follow the same advice given for swelling.

Craving Sweets: Eating sweets only makes you want more sweets. Since most sweet foods aren't particularly nourishing, it's a good idea to avoid getting caught in a cycle where you're popping candy, cookies, and cake into your mouth day after day. When you feel like a chocolate bar, bite into an apple instead. If you feel like attacking a cheesecake, spread some peanut butter on a slice of whole wheat toast, top it with some banana slices, and see if your desire for cake disappears after that. When you get an urge for cookies, substitute plain popcorn.

Being Crabby and Blue: You may find it helpful to talk with a friend; head outdoors for a walk, bike ride, or run; or get your mind off yourself by reading, going to the movies, or doing some artwork, carpentry, or sewing. When it comes down to it, though, there may be nothing you can do about those moods other than reminding yourself that they'll pass in a day or two.

If none of these suggestions work to ease your cramps or depression, see your doctor as soon as possible.

Makeup

Easy Does It

A lot of adults (your parents included?) don't think it's appropriate for anyone under fifteen or sixteen to wear makeup. If you dare to try out a little color on your lips, eyes, or cheeks, they get all excited. Maybe they say you look silly or trashy. And maybe they have a point.

Nothing is more attractive than natural beauty, which is what you get from eating the right foods, getting daily exercise, and making sure you're well rested. Makeup should be used to accentuate what's already there — not to cover it like a mask.

It's easy to go overboard when you're just starting out with makeup, especially if you try to follow the advice you find in most magazines. They usually tell you to put blusher on top of contour powder, on top of toner, on top of base. Then they'll tell you to use a dozen shades of liner and shadow, until your own fresh skin is buried under a coat of cosmetics.

For most occasions other than Halloween, the *effect* of the makeup should show, but not the makeup itself. It takes years of practice to make a lot of makeup look like a little, so you're better off using just enough to highlight your best features and give a little shape and sparkle to your face.

The basics:

o blush powder (pick a shade that blends to look natural; otherwise you may find people asking how you got that rash on your face)
o mascara (black if you have dark skin or hair, brown if you're fair)
o lip color (use just enough to brighten up your face, not so much that your mouth screams "LIPSTICK")

For special occasions:

o foundation or base (as close to your natural skin tone as possible)
o eyeliner pencil (same rules as mascara)

○ eye shadow (choose quiet, earthy shades — remember, they're supposed to play up your eyes, not outshine them)

Before you spend your entire allowance on cosmetics, remember that you're just blowing money if you expect makeup alone to make you look your best. All of the liner, mascara, and shadow in the world won't do a thing for eyes that lack the genuine sparkle you get from good health. Powders, blush, and foundation are wasted on skin that isn't well nourished.

Also, don't fall for makeup, creams, and shampoos that claim to contain various vitamins, proteins, and other nutrients. Nutrients work for you from the inside out. The protein from the fish, legumes, eggs, lean meats, and yogurt you eat is what nourishes your hair — not the protein that's added to shampoos or conditioners. And if you want your skin to benefit from vitamins, eat fresh fruits and vegetables instead of relying on soaps and face creams with vitamins added.

In other words, the place to start for the look you want is the supermarket, not the makeup counter.

Caring for Your Skin

How you remove your makeup and care for your skin matters just as much as how well you put it on. Unless you get every bit of makeup off your face, it will attract dirt and bacteria, which

Facials

If you want to treat yourself and your skin, give yourself a facial. It's not only good for you, it feels terrific. You can make a facial from ordinary household goods. Here are three of them.

❈ Honey Facial

1 tablespoon honey
1 egg yolk
1 teaspoon olive oil

Beat the egg yolk with a fork. Add the oil and blend well. Add the honey, using a spoon that you've rinsed with hot water.
Stir it until it's all blended together.
Smear it on your face and leave it for fifteen minutes. Rinse off.

❈ Cucumber Facial

1 cucumber
½ teaspoon lemon juice
1 teaspoon witch hazel (you can find it at any drugstore)
1 egg white, beaten with an electric beater until it's fluffy.

Peel the cucumber and run it through a blender or food

will lead to zits. Also, old makeup builds up into a shadow that keeps your new makeup from looking as good as it could.

Along with your makeup, buy a cleanser (with a

processor. Pour the cucumber pulp into a colander or strainer, and force it through, catching the liquid that comes out in a bowl underneath.

Combine the liquid from the cucumber with the lemon juice and witch hazel.

Stir it and add the beaten egg white.
Put it on your face and leave it for fifteen minutes or more.
Rinse off.

❁ Parsley Facial

1 bunch of parsley
1 cup distilled water (you can find it at the supermarket)
1 tablespoon honey
1 egg yolk

Boil the parsley in the distilled water for fifteen minutes.
Pour the water out through a strainer or colander, catching it in a bowl underneath.
Let the water cool, then add the honey.
Beat the egg yolk with a fork, then add it, too.
Pat the mixture onto your face, and leave it for fifteen minutes.
Rinse off.

moisturizer if you need one), and get a mild soap (not an acne or deodorant soap) to use afterward. Whenever you wash your face, use warm water to loosen the dirt, then rinse with cold.

Seeing a Doctor

Like most people, you can probably think of better ways to pass the time than having a physical examination. But regular checkups are important to ensure good health and spot any problems quickly. Once you're at the doctor's office, there's plenty you can do to make it both interesting and worthwhile for yourself.

Choose a Doctor Who's Good for You

It's important to be honest when you discuss your health with your doctor. If you don't trust your doctor, if you're uncomfortable asking questions or answering them truthfully, find another doctor. Maybe you've been seeing the same one since you were a baby, and you haven't really thought about whether you like this particular doctor. Maybe you think of the doctor as an extension of your parents and haven't really thought about seeing a doctor who would treat you as an individual instead of merely your parents' kid.

You should be comfortable enough with him or her to bring up your most personal concerns. If that means finding a new doctor, ask your friends how they feel about theirs, and try to see one of the people they recommend. Or make an appoint-

ment at the adolescent or teenage health clinic at a
hospital near you.

Contrary to what you may have heard, all doctors are *not* the same. Some speed through an examination, barely taking time to ask you how
you're feeling. Others carefully explain what
they're doing and finding as they go along. They
ask you everything from how things are going in
school to what you're eating for breakfast these
days. The worst doctors make you feel that going
for a physical is like taking a shirt to the clean-
ers — you just leave your body there to have
some work done. The best doctors make you feel
that you're helping them provide care for you.
They give you enough information, guidance, and
support so you can take responsibility for keeping
yourself healthy.

Ask Questions

Your doctor knows that you haven't had the
benefit of several years of medical school; she or
he won't think you're dumb for wanting to know
what's happening with your body or what will be
done to you during the examination. In fact, most
doctors believe that answering your questions is
part of their job. They know that it's especially
important now, when your body is changing; you
should understand what to expect, and what's normal or not normal.

What kinds of questions? Anything at all that
has to do with the way you've been feeling and

developing. You might want to know why everyone else at school is taller than you are, or why your period hasn't started yet, as well as what to expect when it does. You might want to know whether or not you're too fat, and what you can do about your weight if there is something wrong with it. Maybe you've noticed that one breast is growing faster than the other and you want to know why. You might have some questions about birth control.

Start thinking about your questions several days before your examination, and take a list of them along with you when you go.

Ask for Your History

Your history is the record of events in your health and development. Your doctor should have a record of it in his or her office. This information is bound to come in handy for you sooner or later, like when you're transferring to a new school, applying for work, or going to summer camp. Besides, the more you know about your physical history, the better equipped you'll be to take responsibility for yourself.

Get a Copy of Your Yellow Card

This card should list all of the vaccinations you've had since you were born. Even though your parents probably have a copy, you should have your own in case you need it when your folks aren't around. Take it with you whenever you travel or stay somewhere away from home. You can't tell when you might have to know if you've been vaccinated against a particular disease.

Be Ready to Answer Your Doctor's Questions

The most important question your doctor will ask — if your periods have started — is "What was the *first* day of your most recent period?" Your doctor has to know this in order to get a good idea of what's happening with your body. By knowing that date, your doctor can tell which hormones are likely to be in your system during the examination. Since hormones have so much to do with how your body operates, knowing which ones are there will enable your doctor to have a more complete picture of how you're functioning.

Your doctor will also want to know the name of every medication you're taking. Copy the name straight off the bottle, and jot down the dosage, too.

It's Up to You

Even if your doctor says you're in fine health, don't let the good news convince you there's no need to work on improving it.

To your doctor, being in good health may mean only that you're free from disease, and that you're growing and developing as you should.

There's no doubt that this is important. But for you to be at your *best,* good health must mean more to you than simply not being sick.

The good health that comes from eating well, exercising often, and dealing with your problems lets you make the most of you and everything you do. It comes from making good choices for your body and mind — every day — and from remembering that those choices will affect how you look and feel today *and* in the years ahead. It's your body — take charge!

Bibliography

To learn more about . . .

Your Developing Body
BodyWorks: The Kids' Guide to Food and Physical Fitness,
by Carol Bershad and Deborah Bernick. Random House,
1981.
  Really fun-to-read introduction to what it takes to stay fit.

Changing Bodies, Changing Lives, by Ruth Bell *et al.* Random House, 1981.
  What's happening with your body and how it affects other
parts of your life.

*Don't Worry, You're Normal: A Teenagers' Guide to Self-
Health,* by Nissa Simon. Thomas Crowell, 1982.
  Clear, simple, and reassuring explanations of what's hap-
pening with your body, and advice for how to keep it well.

The New Our Bodies, Ourselves, by the Boston Women's
Health Book Collective. Simon and Schuster, 1985.
  Detailed discussions of sexual development and other as-
pects of womanhood.

The Teenage Body Book, by Kathy McCoy and Charles Wibbelsman. Simon and Schuster, 1984.
    Answers just about any question you could have about your physical and emotional development.

Your Body Is Trying to Tell You Something, by Richard Stiller. Harcourt Brace Jovanovich, 1979.
    How your body lets you know that something's wrong, and how you can learn to respond.

Sexuality
Changing Bodies, Changing Lives, by Ruth Bell *et al.* Random House, 1981.
    What's happening with your body and how it affects other parts of your life.

It Won't Happen to Me, by Paula McGuire. Delacorte, 1983.
    Interviews with teenagers who became pregnant "by accident." For every girl who's having sex or thinking she might.

Sex and Birth Control: A Guide for the Young, by E. James Lieberman and Ellen Peck. Thomas Crowell, 1981.
    A very thorough and clear discussion of sexuality and contraception.

The Teenage Body Book, by Kathy McCoy and Charles Wibbelsman. Simon and Schuster, 1984.
    Answers just about any question you could have about your physical and emotional development.

Food, Nutrition, and Weight Control
Fat Free: Common Sense for Young Weight Worriers, by Sara Gilbert. Macmillan, 1978.
    An excellent introduction to weight control. This book of-

fers several ways to determine if you are too fat, as well as some helpful and supportive advice for what to do if it turns out that you are.

Food, Nutrition, and You, by Linda Peavy and Ursula Smith. Charles Scribner's Sons, 1982.
Combines basic information, good advice, and amusing anecdotes from the history of food.

Going Vegetarian: A Guide for Teenagers, by Sada Fretz. William Morrow, 1983.
Reasons to "go vegetarian," how to plan and prepare nutritious, scrumptious meatless meals, and superb, simple recipes to get you started.

The Woman Doctor's Diet for Teenage Girls, by Barbara Edelstein. Ballantine, 1981.
A diet that's sensible and safe, plus a good discussion of the role that food plays in your life, and help in changing the attitudes toward food that may be making you fat.

Movement and Exercise
Jane Fonda's Workout Book, by Jane Fonda. Simon and Schuster, 1981.
Effective exercise routines and pep talks to help you through them.

Sportspower, by Ralph L. Carnes and Valerie Carnes. St. Martin's Press, 1983.
How to put more into and get more out of the sports that you do.

Stretching, by Bob Anderson. Shelter Publications, 1980.
The *right* way to warm up. Easy-to-follow and fun-to-do stretching exercises.

The Young Athletes' Health Handbook, by Douglas Jackson and Susan Pescar. Everest House, 1981.
Lots of tips for choosing a sport, caring for injuries, handling competition, and developing stamina and strength.

Stress and Emotional Problems
Bulimia, by Janice M. Cauwels. Doubleday, 1983.
About one girl's recovery from a serious eating disorder.

The Kids' Book about Parents, by the Children of the Fayerweather Street School and Eric E. Rofes. Houghton Mifflin, 1984.
Written with the idea that understanding your parents is the best way to get along with them.

Starving for Attention, by Cherry Boone O'Neill. Continuum, 1982.
The author tells how she struggled with, then recovered from, anorexia nervosa.

Teenage Stress, by Daniel Cohen and Susan Cohen. Evans, 1984.
What stress feels like, what causes it, and what you can do about it.

The Teenage Survival Guide, by Kathy McCoy. Simon and Schuster, 1981.
Deals with just about every problem that can come up in your life, and offers good, supportive advice for coping with them.

Staying Well and Looking Good
Doctor Zizmor's Guide to Clearer Skin, by Dr. Jonathan Zizmor and Diane English. Lippincott, 1980.
Terrific advice for clearing up your complexion.

Drugs and You, by Arnold Madison. Julian Messner, 1982.
How drugs affect the way you feel and function.

The Stop Smoking Book for Teens, by Curtis W. Casewit.
Julian Messner, 1980.
"Why you smoke, why you shouldn't, how to stop."

The Teenage Body Book, by Kathy McCoy and Charles
Wibbelsman. Simon and Schuster, 1984.
Answers just about any question you could have about
your physical and emotional development.